WALL
JOB PRIMER

A Comprehensive Guide for Those Aspiring to Work in Financial Services

- Industry overview in layman terms
- Investment banks, money managers, hedge funds and the jobs within
- Chapter 5 dedicated exclusively to **quantitative roles** in the industry
- Strategies and insights for landing jobs and maximizing success (including compensation!)

Aaron Brask, PHD

ISBN: 1453889280
ISBN-13: 9781453889282

Contents

Acknowledgements

There have been many family members, friends and colleagues who have significantly impacted my career and the writing of this book. Hopefully I have spared them much agony by excluding them from direct involvement with this book.

My family has always supported of my endeavors no matter how odd they appear at times. A special thanks to my mom, dad, brother and sister for their love and encouragement throughout my life.

I am very thankful to two of my best friends, Alex More and William Jo, who lured me into finance. Alex was the first person to tell me about quants on Wall Street. I benefited enormously from his advice as I transitioned from Florida to New York as he had done several years before. William's entrepreneurial spirit has always encouraged me and I will surely knock on his door more than once as I enter a new and more entrepreneurial phase of my own life.

Befriending Brian Alvers during my university years was truly a blessing. I am not sure I would have survived some of our classes with my sanity intact had it not been for his humorous anecdotes. I benefited greatly from his insights on the actuarial profession which he ultimately pursued.

To all of the teachers and professors from whom I've had the honor to learn throughout my academic career, I am eternally grateful. Ms. Terry Lambert provided me with solid mathematical foundations throughout high school. At university, Dr. Bruce Edwards' enthusiasm and experience made learning fun and practical. Dr. Douglas Cenzer's goal setting helped me through my first real challenge in the mathematics curriculum. Dr. Nicolae Dinculeanu and Dr. Neil White both demonstrated to me and other students that mathematics can be taught with class and eloquence. Dr. Joseph Glover initiated and taught a course in financial mathematics which opened my eyes to this exciting new area. I am thankful for his sound guidance and immeasurable patience as my advisor while I worked through my dissertation.

I have also been lucky to work with and for several people who have been instrumental in shaping my career. Jim Cohen was the unlucky first person who first had to extract some sort of financial utility out of me in a professional workplace. Lucky for me, Jim was incredibly easy to work for and I learned a great deal about proprietary trading and risk management from him.

Charles Monet, the man who first hired me to work on Wall Street, has my utmost respect and gratitude. I believe the projects he had our team focus on were truly visionary endeavors and are still at the cutting edge of Wall Street's attempts to manage risk, especially in the area of correlation.

I benefited greatly from moving to London and working with Peter Allen. Amongst other things, I learned more about presentation style and attention to detail from him than anyone else. Stephen Einchcomb also enhanced my London transition with his healthy doses of cynicism at all the right times.

Luke Olsen and Robert McAdie helped me immensely as I stepped into a more senior role building and managing a global team. Luke always made his helpful and objective advice easily accessible. Robert led by example following his strong convictions even when the tide was against him.

I am thankful to most everyone I worked with throughout my career, especially those with whom I worked closest and those who worked for me; they had to endure all my moods. Abhinandan Deb and Min Tang are two of the smartest individuals I had the pleasure to work with. I benefited greatly from their intellectual firepower. Priya Balasubramanian and Colin Bennett helped me grow and learn to view many concepts from new angles. I am grateful to all of them and wish them all the very best.

Last but not least is my loving wife, Stephanie. She is a great source of strength and always helps me keep my life in focus.

Preface

This book is written under the assumption that the reader has minimal prior knowledge of the financial industry. The original reason I decided to write this book is that I wanted to better prepare anyone with quantitative educational backgrounds for careers in finance, not just the rocket science *quants*[1]. This was mostly born out of the fact that I wish I had had something similar when I started my own career. Despite my original intentions to make this specific to the quantitative community, it later became clear that most of what I wrote was applicable to anyone getting into finance.

As a result of this epiphany, I concentrated the quant specific content in Chapter 5 to keep the rest of the content universal. This is there where I elaborate on a variety of roles that require varying degrees of quant skills. Background information on the financial industry comprises the first three chapters, the fourth chapter describes actual jobs, and the insights/strategies presented in Chapter 6 are critically important for anyone considering working in the financial industry.

Entering the financial industry can be very challenging, especially when it comes to the top investment banks and investment firms (eg, hedge funds). Many complain that these institutions are the exclusive domain of Ivy League and PhD graduates and that they do not give all comers a fair chance[2]. While I have seen this favoritism in practice from both sides (trying to get hired and

---

[1]   Many people assume that the definition of a *quant* is someone who possesses a mathematics, physics, or similarly technical PhD. As such, most all of the content regarding *quant* careers is not applicable for the broader quantitative who do not have PhDs. My goal was to target the entire quantitative community (say, anyone who is particularly inclined to mathematics and chose to pursue a degree in a technical discipline) as there are many quantitative roles within the financial industry that do not require PhDs.

[2]   This may be an inevitable reality. Recruiting personnel in this industry have to filter the massive piles of applications and resumes that they receive. With few other tools at their disposal, they implicitly rely on the selection processes of these Ivy League institutions and their educational programs as a tool to narrow their own search for quality candidates. In fact, I would argue that it is naïve to assume that your resumes will be read in full once submitted.

hiring) and can confirm this bias exists, my own experience proves that it is possible to get onto Wall Street without an Ivy League degree. Even more encouraging, I observed many other non-Ivy Leaguers and non-PhDs land great jobs in the industry.

Even for those that get their foot in the door, there is much to look out for. Understanding the bigger picture and the internal dynamics is critical to the degree of your success. Compensation, for example, attracts many bright people to this industry. However, while many perform very well on the job, their naïveté lands them on the lower side of the compensation scale.

This book is organized into 6 chapters. The first three chapters are intended to educate the reader on the world of finance. Chapter 1 presents a brief introduction to capital markets, describing the roles that banks and some other financial institutions play. Chapter 2 starts to break down the anatomy of an investment bank in particular, its different organs and their individual functions. Chapter 3 describes many of the institutions (collectively known as the *buy-side*) that invest money on behalf of others and utilize investment banking services in the process.

Chapter 4 builds upon the industry overview of the first three chapters and delves into specific job descriptions for a variety of roles. I then present a scoring system based on 10 attributes that are critical in assessing the suitability of these roles for different candidates. This scoring system targets both the prerequisite skill sets but also the characteristics of the roles that make them more or less compatible with different people.

Chapter 5 identifies and explains the roles that specifically require quantitative backgrounds. While Chapter 5 is geared towards the quantitative community, it is also helpful for others to read as most other roles deal directly with these quant roles. Conversely, it is critical that quants read the other chapters as well.

The topics in Chapter 6 are essential reading for most everyone in, or aspiring to be in, the financial services industry. Chapter 6 turned out to be much longer than I originally intended. Its content is relatively independent of the previous five chapters and, like the first four chapters, the content is universal. Chapter 6 contains important guidelines for landing a good job (searching for openings, resumes, interviewing, and soliciting offers) and making the most of your role once you get your foot in the door (working with a new manager, leveraging resources, politics, promotions and compensation - page **96** for those who want skip to that).

The bottom line underscoring these insights and strategies is that there are many pitfalls and gravitational pulls within any work environment. You are much better off being aware of them and being able to navigate accordingly. I attempt to relay those which I have identified throughout my own career and found to be most important.

Lastly, there are several sections in the appendix where I elaborate on some concepts mentioned in the book. The only reason they are placed in the appendix is that I felt they might dilute the content and distract the reader from the point at hand within the text. And then there is the very last section in the appendix that describes my own trajectory; it starts with me anxiously wondering what math majors could do for a living and then explains how I got onto Wall Street myself.

Thank you for reading. I would be very grateful for any and all feedback on the book including its structure, content, writing style, highlighted resources, etc. Feel free to email me at aaronbrask@gmail.com.

Chapter 1:

A Quick Overview of Capital Markets

1.1 Raising Capital

As with every *market*, there are two sides: buyers and sellers. In the financial markets, there are those who have *capital* (money) they would like to invest (ie, buyers) and there are those who want capital (ie, sellers). For capital markets, we are generally talking about large sums of money and can simplify matters by thinking of the sellers as being corporations and the buyers as institutional investors managing, say, hundreds of millions or even billions of dollars on the behalf of many other parties who have given them their money (eg, mutual funds).

Naturally, these investors want a return on their investment, and with minimal risk. Generally speaking, higher risk investments often boast higher returns to compensate for the risk. But given the large number of diverse corporations and different types of securities (eg, stocks and bonds being the most common), it can be a daunting task to determine which investments offer the best balance of risk and return. Even a seemingly simple decision to lend money and earn interest from another party requires significant due diligence.

Starting small, we can easily imagine that individuals need to borrow some money for one of a number of reasons. They could simply want to buy a car, attend a university, buy a house, etc. In most situations like these, the local bank or credit union is capable of assessing the situation and providing the capital if they believe the risk/reward balance is favorable. In particular, they want to be sure that if they lend the money out, there will be a high probability that they will get it back along with enough interest to be profitable. So they must account for the interest rates they are paying their depositors (that is where they get the money from), the probability of not getting paid back, and something extra so that they can make a profit.

In order to assess the probability of not getting paid back, the bank will look into the applicant's credit and earnings history. That is, they will look at the history of the applicant's repayment or defaulting on previous loans and the stability of their earnings. The more they have borrowed and repaid on time, the better their credit history or rating will be. In this case, the bank would be more inclined to lend the applicant money at a proper interest rate. In the case where there were some blemishes on the applicant's credit record, the loan may be offered with a higher interest rate to compensate for the extra risk, or simply be turned down.

Ratcheting up a few notches, large corporations are not dissimilar. They also have many different reasons for seeking capital; they might want money to expand their own business line(s), ride out a difficult economic period, or acquire some new assets (eg, competitors, suppliers, or other businesses). Just as with loans to individual people, corporations will be assessed in terms of their ability to repay the loans.

Figure 1: Means of Capital Raising for Large Corporations

	BORROW	SELL OWNERSHIP
Private	**Bank loan** - Direct loan to company from a bank - Generally higher interest rate - Avoid regulatory filings	**Private equity** - Sell stake to group of private investors - Potentially lose management autonomy - Avoid regulatory filings
Public	**Bond issue** - Money comes from the investing public - Generally lower interest rate - Requires public filings	**IPO or share sale** - Money comes from the investing public - More autonomous terms - Requires public filings

It is worth noting that large corporations generally have a few more options available to them for raising capital. In particular, they might also be able to borrow the money from the investing public via selling (issuing) a bond or they could sell a stake in their company to raise money instead. Selling ownership of the company could be to a private group of investors or to the public via an initial public offering (IPO) of shares. Figure 1 above illustrates these by breaking them down into four choices based on two factors: the decision between borrowing or selling ownership and the choice of a public or private deal. Figure 1 also lists some factors associated with their choices for different means of capital raising (more on this in Chapter 2).

1.2 Capital Structure

The norm is for large corporations to fund themselves (ie, raise capital) via more than just one of the ways we discussed above. They can also use variations on these themes such as preferred shares, convertible bonds, perpetuities, hybrids, etc). The ultimate combination of funding sources is called the company's *capital structure*, though it often refers to the one dimensional balance between debt (borrowing) and equity (ownership), not the private/public distinction. The capital structure is a, if not the, primary consideration large corporations will make when deciding on how to raise capital. There are positives and negatives to both equity and debt, but one overriding constraint is maintaining the ability to pay the debt (interest and principal) back, and on time.

If a company runs into trouble and does not repay its loans or debts on time, the company is said to have *defaulted*. In this case, the company's ownership transitions from the equity stakeholders to the creditors and the value of the equity (stock) should go to zero. There is a priority system in place whereby some creditors are more *senior* to others and will get paid back first or have entitlement to specific company assets (ie, collateral against the borrowed money). The debt that is farther back in this priority system is said to be *subordinated*. In general, loans are more senior than bonds and bonds are more senior than equity, so loans and bondholders get repaid before shareholders.

It may seem unfair that the shareholders end up with the short end of the stick in a default, but it is the natural pecking order in this unfortunate situation. It is the fortunate case where the company thrives that balances this relationship out. When the company does very well, the shareholders typically benefit more than the lenders because once the lenders are paid back, all of the leftover profits are owned by the shareholders. In other words, the shareholders have unlimited upside while the lenders' upside is limited to getting their money back plus some interest. Accordingly, it is left to the markets to decide whether the price of the debt is appropriately priced relative to the equity. Chapter 4 discusses this specific topic in more depth.

The more debt there is relative to equity, the more *leverage* the company is using. Leverage often has a negative stigma attached to it, but it is not always bad. For someone who is starting or expanding a company and is confident in its success, they might not want to relinquish any of their ownership. So borrowing money via a loan or debt issue might be the best solution. Once the borrowed money is paid back, there is no further obligation and ownership of all of the future profits remains intact. In addition to this preference, there is a tax related benefit that comes from using debt/loans: interest payments are tax deductible. As a result, most large corporations have a significant amount of debt in their capital structure.

Figure 2: Simplified Depiction of Two Generic *Capital Structures*

LEVERAGED COMPANY		NON-LEVERAGED COMPANY	
Assets	**Liabilities**	**Assets**	**Liabilities**
Cash and cash equivalents	**Debt**	Cash and cash equivalents	**Debt**
...	→ More debt / less equity	...	
Physical assets	→ More interest to pay	Physical assets	Equity
...	→ More risk of default	...	
Intangible assets		Intangible assets	→ Less debt / more equity
			→ less interest to pay
	Equity		→ less risk of default

This might tempt the question of why a company would not always just borrow money in order to get this tax benefit and maintain 100% ownership. However, too much debt can burden a company in that it will have an obligation to make the interest payments on a predetermined schedule, regardless of whether the company is doing well or not at the time. Consequently, the stability of the cash flows generated by the company – that would be relied upon to repay interest – is another factor CEOs and CFOs use to determine the appropriate capital structure for their company. A company with very reliable cash flow can take on more debt and benefit from the above factors. A company with less reliable cash flows will generally prefer to have less debt in order to create a buffer between the amount of money it expects to generate and how much it has to pay in interest. This helps protect the company against defaulting should they incur a shortfall relative to their business performance expectations. There are also several other important considerations for new and established companies to make when choosing amongst different means of capital raising and we discuss those in the next chapter.

1.3 The Role of Investment Banks

In order for most corporations to issue bonds or equity to the public, they generally employ an investment bank to facilitate the transaction. The distribution channels investment banks have in place are critically important for corporations seeking to raise capital. Investment banks generally have groups of marketing and sales people that have relationships with institutional investors who can purchase significant stakes (debt or equity) in new or expanding companies. In any case, it would be difficult for a company to sell its shares directly to the public[3]. The process by which banks manage these transactions is called *underwriting*. Interestingly, banks will often purchase their own stake in the equity or debt being issued. This is both a nice gesture to the corporation and a positive signal to potential investors.

Because investment banks are coordinating transactions directly between investors and the corporations for their capital raising, these are called *primary markets*. The bankers who work on these transaction are often said to work in *capital markets* divisions. Knowing the value of their distribution networks, banks charge hefty fees to corporations who use them to raise capital. IPOs can be quite expensive as banks rake in fees between 3-7% of the notional being sold; bond sales are cheaper at around 1-3% of the notional. Larger (multibillion dollar) and more vanilla deals are generally done at the lower end of the fee range (in terms of %), but innovative and more complex financing solutions are often rewarded with fees at the higher end of the range (eg, convertible bonds or other hybrid securities).

---

3   The initial public offering of GOOGLE was an interesting case in that they essentially bypassed their banks' distribution channels and setup an online auction where any investor, however large or small, could be a part of the IPO. Given that the price ended up at the low end of expectations and the subsequent huge rally (issued at $85/share and rallied to $XXX/share within NN months), it could be argued that their different approach might have intimidated some large investors who might have otherwise participated and bid the price higher. On the other hand, their IPO strategy was remarkably brave and innovative. It could set a precedent for other companies to bypass investment banks' control over the process which has been mired in controversy as accusations of price fixing and preferential treatment (giving low priced IPO issues to favored clients) have plagued the process.

1.4 Secondary Markets and Derivatives

Once securities[4] are public (ie, after an IPO or debt issue), investors can buy and sell them via banks or brokers. These are called *secondary markets*. In order to facilitate liquidity (the ease with which investors can buy and sell), investment banks will *make markets* in most of the biggest stock and bond securities. In other words, they will agree to provide bid and ask prices for those securities so that investors will always have a place to buy/sell the securities. Banks also generally offer derivatives[5] (eg, calls or puts) on these securities which can be used for many different purposes such as leverage, risk management, or creating new types of structured products.

Within a bank, the business lines are generally divided amongst the types of securities they trade (ie, buy and sell). So there would be individual business units for equities, bonds, currencies, commodities, etc. Each business line would likely deal in its own and related securities (including derivatives on those securities) though can be some overlap. Within each business line, there will generally be two key divisions: sales and trading. The sales force will bring in deals or transactions which trading will execute. In order to generate more transactions, some banks also have research divisions for various products they trade so that the sales force can more easily approach clients and suggest ideas for them to transact. More sophisticated businesses will often have structuring teams who try to innovate and create new or customized products (generally derivatives) for clients. We will discuss these roles in more detail in the next chapter.

1.5 The Buy-side

The term *buy-side* is a broad label which generally describes financial institutions that utilize the different services that banks and brokerages offer (eg, research, execution, prime brokerage, market making, derivatives, etc). In this context, the banks and brokerages are labeled as the *sell-side* as they sell their services to the buy-side.

---

4   The term *security* broadly refers to any sort of ownership or debt related to a company or some assets. For simplicity, it is easiest to think of securities as being a generalized description of stocks and/or bonds.

5   We explain the concept of derivatives in the appendix. In a nutshell, a derivative is a financial instrument that derives its value from another security. Futures and options are very common derivatives, for example.

Much of the buy-side comprises for-profit companies whose sole purpose is to take other people's money and invest it on their behalf; these are generally called *asset managers*. One relatively common example is a mutual fund. Other buy-side institutions have large pools of money that they must invest for different purposes. Pension funds and insurance companies are the two largest examples. Both strive to make investments that will ensure they can fulfill future liabilities. For pension funds, private and public, these liabilities are defined by the retirement plans promised to their clients. For insurance companies, these liabilities include a complex combination of potential insurance claims as well as payoffs defined by the financial products they sell to their clients.

Most asset managers are specialized in terms of their focus — equity, fixed income, real estate, commodities, etc — or have individual arms dealing with specific asset classes. Yet there are some which classify themselves as multi-strategy and invest across asset classes. There are a wide variety of buy-side firms that employ many different strategies and we describe these firms in Chapter 3.

1.6 Exchanges and Clearinghouses

While not central to this text, exchanges and clearinghouses play a large enough part within the financial markets that it is worth understanding their role. Exchanges and clearinghouses facilitate the execution and settlement of different securities for their members. Their members are brokers — institutions who execute trades for their clients. These can be standalone or subsidiaries of investment banks. Indeed, most large investment banks operate such businesses as it is often considered a critical element of their franchise which complements the rest of their business. It is worth noting that the execution of client orders is done on an *agency basis* from the exchanges' perspective. That is, the exchange itself does not take the other side of the transaction as happens with market making businesses. Nevertheless, exchanges employ[6] traders to buy and sell for their own accounts and facilitate liquidity in the securities being traded on the exchange.

Exchanges sit between buyers and sellers so that both the buyer and the seller face the exchange as their counterparty, not each other. This mitigates

---

6   The word *employ* is slightly misleading in the sense that these traders actually pay the exchange for the opportunity to trade their securities.

counterparty risk as the exchange, being backed by its members, is more creditworthy than its members or any of their clients. In order for the exchange to protect itself from counterparty risk, it imposes a margining or collateral system on those with whom it deals. These members, in turn, impose similar margining and collateral requirements on their clients.

Once transactions are executed on an exchange, its clearinghouse(s) will ensure that the monies and securities are transferred within the allotted time frame. The timeline for cash payments are generally stipulated via the convention "T+1", "T+2", etc. when the cash is due in the sellers account 1, 2, etc days after the transaction is executed.

1.7 Different Types of Banks

Before Chapter 2 delves into the components of an *investment* bank, it makes sense to take a step back and review the different types of banks and their activities. Many banks today comprise different banking operations under a single holding company and attempt to present a unified bank, with a single name, to their clients. As a result, delineations between different types of banks may appear blurred to the outsider. We break banks into four primary categories: retail, private, commercial, and investment banks.

1.7.1 Retail Banks

Retail banks are probably the most well known of all as they are the banks used by most of the public for everyday banking needs. They offer their clients a variety of services including storing and retrieving their money, writing checks, taking out loans, credit cards, as well as some basic means of investing (eg, certificates of deposit). The traditional strategy by which retail banks operate is twofold. First, they pay interest in order to attract deposits. Then they lend money out after conducting due diligence as to the creditworthiness of borrowers. The interest they charge the borrower is higher than they pay their depositors, thus allowing them to pay for their operations and hopefully some profit in the process.

1.7.2 Private Banks[7]

Private banks primarily cater to wealthy individuals and families. These clients are often referred to as HNWIs (high-net-worth-individuals) or UNHWIs

---

7   Historically, the term *private bank* simply referred to an unincorporated banking institution. Now, however, it describes an institution which is geared towards more personal service for wealthy clients.

(ultra-HNWIs). Private banks do not attempt to compete with retail banks. Their services (eg, investments, tax planning, financing) tend to be more sophisticated and customized for their individual clients' needs.

It is worth noting that private banks have sometimes been cast in a negative light as a result of their reputation for secrecy. Some private banks, notably Swiss, have made secrecy a primary selling point with their clients. Accordingly, governments around the globe are cracking down on this banking secrecy as it relates to tax evasion. Nevertheless, structuring investments to complement a client's specific tax situation will likely remain a popular practice. Areas such as estate planning and investment gains are intrinsically linked with taxes.

1.7.3 Commercial Banks

Just as with individuals, businesses have banking needs and these needs are catered to by commercial banks. Some of the basic cash services such as checking/savings accounts and loans work more or less in the same way, but bank dealings with businesses naturally involve larger sums and require some specialized services. One such example would be *lines of credit*. Businesses will often open *lines of credit* with their bank, enabling them to borrow more quickly when the needs arises at a later time as opposed to waiting to complete an application process. Other commercial services include payment processing and foreign exchange. Most large companies require scalable systems to process their large number of payments and multi-national companies often require foreign exchange services to manage different currencies.

There are other interpretations or definitions of what a commercial bank is. Some of these overlap with our description of retail banks; others overlap with our description of investment banks. In any case, our description of a commercial bank aligns with the more traditional definition and is the more commonly used.

1.7.4 Investment Banks

Investment banks generally deal with large corporations and institutional investors, though they also work with governments and municipalities. As we described in the capital markets section, investment banks can help corporations with mergers and acquisitions, capital raising, and other market related services. And they service institutional investors with their sales, trading and research facilities. The next chapter is devoted to specifically to describing an investment bank and all of its components in detail.

Figure 3: Different Types of Banks

BANK	NON-LEVERAGED COMPANY
Retail bank	Deals primarily with individuals. Main function is to take deposits and make loans but also facilitate other basic financial services the average individual might utilize (eg, credit cards).
Private bank	Exclusive retail bank that only deals with HNWIs and UHNWIs (high net worth individuals and ultra HNWIs). While some private banks (PBs) might have made secrecy a primary selling point, PBs generally advise and help their clients invest money via third party (ie, independent) asset managers. They also often liaise with other institutions (eg, banks) that offer custom or structured (ie, derivative) investments that are not available to the average investor.
Commercial bank	Takes deposits and makes loans for medium to large sized corporations just as retail banks do for individuals. Provide lines of credit and foreign exchange services.
Investment bank	Deals with large corporations and institutional investors. Advise on M&A and execute capital raising for corporations. Provide markets (buy and sell) and research in securities and derivatives for institutional asset managers.

Chapter 1 Concepts

- Means of raising capital: Loan vs equity, private vs public
- Capital structure and leverage
- Investments banks' intermediary role in primary markets
- Secondary markets and derivatives
- Buy-side and sell-side
- Exchanges and clearing houses
- Different types of banks

Chapter 2:

Anatomy of an Investment Bank

As discussed in chapter one, most large banks integrate multiple types of banks and business lines via a common holding company. Figure 4 below outlines a generic structure for such a bank holding company. Each of these business lines is generally run independently as to avoid potential conflicts of interest[8], though some economies of scale and synergies are utilized where possible.

Figure 4: Generic Bank Holding Company and its Primary Divisions

BANK HOLDING COMPANY			
Retail bank	**Commercial bank**	**Investment bank**	**Investment mgt.**
- Service individuals	- Service corporations	- Service corporations and institutional investors	- Invest money on behalf of clients
- Checking, saving, loans, etc	- Treasury and payment processing services	- Capital raising and advisory	- Manage multiple funds with different investment objectives
- Credit card services	- Cash management, loans, etc	- Sales, trading, research, brokerage	

The generic illustration above only contains four divisions that might be integrated in a bank holding company. We believe these to be the largest and most common amongst large banks, but it should be noted that different banks have various combinations of these and possibly other businesses (eg, private banks, structured fund management, etc).

---

8   Conflicts of interest can arise in many areas of banking and there are many regulations to prevent it. One example might be the corporate financiers or commercial bankers; they are often privy to confidential information about their corporate clients which should not be leaked to the trading division. Another example could be the investment management arms of banks; they might potentially favor their namesake investment banks (or broker/dealer) for services it could otherwise get cheaper elsewhere to the detriment of their clients.

We have already touched on the various business activities of investment management, retail and commercial banks in the first chapter. As the title indicates, this chapter focuses exclusively on the investment banking division. The next chapter describes the buy side, which includes investment management divisions, in more detail.

Figure 5: Primary Investment Banking Divisions

INVESTMENT BANK		
Corporate finance	**Sales/trading/research**	**Brokerage**
- Fee generation via issuance / advisory	- Profits via risk taking	- Focus on margins and commissions
- Issuing new equity and bond securities	- Market making	- Execution, settlement, clearing
- Capital markets distribution	- Structured products	- Risk netting / leverage
- Strategic advisory on M&A, restructuring, takeover defense, etc	- Distribution channels	- Security lending
	- Proprietary trading	- Confirmations and reporting

We divide investment banking activities into three primary components: *corporate finance*, *secondary markets* (aka *sales and trading*), and *brokerage*. Each firm defines and organizes its businesses differently, but these three business lines generally underpin the primary structure of most large investment banks and comprise the bulk of their revenue. Figure 5 above depicts this breakdown and lists some of the activities that take place within each division.

> **Quick comment:** While those who work in any area of an investment bank are technically investment bankers per the literal definition, this label is generally reserved for those who work in corporate finance (capital raising or advisory). Other areas, such as secondary markets/sales and trading, which we discuss later, will generally defer to their more specific role in defining there jobs (eg, broker, traders, etc). In the following, we adhere to this convention and thus refer to corporate finance bankers when we use the term investment banker.

Just as we acknowledged that the above structure is not shared by all investment banks, the same issue applies as we delve deeper into each business division. In fact, we would argue that the commonality in structuring or defining business units becomes increasingly disparate as you look at firms on a finer scale. Accordingly, we reiterate that the organizational structures and definitions of business units we present are not written in stone. We identify the most common structures and definitions used by the leading investment banks, describe where ambiguities arise and explain how our definition compares with other possible characterizations.

One example of such ambiguity is *corporate finance* because it has varying definitions for what activities it spans. Some use this term to label the specific business relating to corporations financing themselves (ie, raising capital). Others use it as a means of describing any activity involving the finances of a corporation. We prefer the latter and broader definition since it is the characterization investment bankers often offer their clients; they want to be the point person for all transactions with their corporate clients. While the name clearly implies *corporate* clients, many public institutions (municipalities, governments, central banks, etc) utilize similar services. In the following, we primarily focus on corporate transactions and services though the reader should be aware that many public institutions are also key clients of investment bank.

2.1 Corporate Finance

The defining factor of this division is essentially its clientele – corporations. It might be useful to think of investment bankers as the point persons for corporate clients to access many of the products offered within the entire bank holding company. Dealing with corporate clients often involves confidential information that could impact the prices of market securities or the behaviors of others in their industry. As a result, they are confined to their own division so that this *inside* information cannot be leaked out to other parties.

In banking jargon, they create a *Chinese wall*[9] (or firewall) that separates these bankers who are dealing with CEOs, CFOs and other executives from other groups that should not be privy to such information(eg, traders and clients). However, bankers in this division often must interact with other divisions. When this is the case, specific precautions are taken to make sure such

---

9   A Chinese wall is not necessarily physical but often is. Bankers working on such deals generally reside in different buildings or on different floors than others. This jargon applies not only to these bankers, but other areas within a firm where people working with sensitive information are isolated from other groups.

communications comply with the associated regulations and policies. Some-times other parties (eg, a trader whose services may be required to execute a transaction) are temporarily brought *over the wall* in order to work on specific deals but are prohibited from acting on or discussing the deals in which they are involved.

In the following, we break the corporate finance division into two business units that correspond to the next two sections: capital raising and advisory services. The first section expands on the capital raising activities we present-ed in Chapter 1. The other section discusses a variety of high level advisory services that bankers provide to their corporate clients.

It should also be noted that we have brushed over one significant detail regard-ing the structure of this part of an investment bank. There is often a top level split between sectors (eg, technology, healthcare, etc) in most large investment banks. These sectors are then generally divided between capital raising and advisory services individually as illustrated in Figure 6. But, as we already rec-ognized, many firms organize themselves differently. For example, smaller firms often do not have the scale to create separate teams for different sectors.

Figure 6: General Structure of Captial Markets and Advisory Services

CAPITAL RAISING AND ADVISORY SERVICES					
Technology		Healthcare		Other sectors	
Capital raising	Advisory services	Capital raising	Advisory services	Capital raising	Advisory services

2.1.1 Capital Raising

As we described in Chapter 1, corporations often require capital for different purposes. There are numerous reasons companies require financing. Below we list some of most important motivations below:

- **Short term cash flow:** Underlying business is healthy but the impend-ing bills/liabilities temporarily require more cash than is available in the near term (eg, payroll).
- **Renewing financing:** A bond or loan is coming due and the company wants to extend it by borrowing again.

- **Expansion/acquisitions:** Increasing the scale of an existing business or replicating it in another region or market. Purchasing new businesses or competitors.
- **Vertical-ization:** Purchasing suppliers and/or distributors for a more vertically integrated business.
- **Share buybacks:** Company wishes to buy some of the shares that it has previously issued to boost the share price[10].
- **Emergency funding/survival:** An unexpected liability surfaces or the core business is sinking and the company scrambles to keep it afloat.

Given the flexibility and different features that can be structured, there are many ways a company can raise capital. Below we expand on Figure 1 from Chapter 1 and list several key methods of financing. For more details on any of these types of financing, we suggest the reader consult the internet or any books that cover corporate finance.

Figure 7: Key Methods of Raising Capital

Equity based	Debt based
→ Initial public offering (IPO)	→ Bond issues (long dated bonds or short term commercial paper)
→ Follow-on offering / secondary placements / Rights issue	→ Leveraged loans (eg, LBO) / high-yield or junk bonds
→ Convertible bonds	→ Mezzanine debt
→ Private placement / venture capital	→ Commercial loans

As we mentioned in Chapter 1, capital structure is often an important driver for large companies deciding between debt and equity. However, there are many other factors companies may consider when deciding precisely what type of financing they should use:

---

10   A share buy-back can boost the corresponding share price in multiple ways. The actual buying naturally provides temporary increased demand for the shares. Buy-backs also often signal that the company believes its shares are cheap. Fewer shares in the market means the earnings will be split amongst fewer parties, increasing the proportional ownership of each.

11   Bankers will generally work with the firm's commerical bank in order to facilitate commercial loans.

- **Accounting considerations:** Companies will consider which type of financing will look the best in their accounts. It is not unheard of for companies to use means of financing that are economically inferior to others simply to make their balance sheet or income statement look better. Naturally there are rules governing what can be done, but this sometimes leads to a cat and mouse game where financial engineering tries to stay one step ahead.
- **Duration:** The length of time the financing is required naturally makes some means of financing more amenable than others. For example, a company that needs cash for its payroll but knows it has cash flow coming in soon may opt for shorter duration securities like commercial paper.
- **Feasibility / speed:** Depending upon the economic climate, investors may or may not be willing to invest via one means or another (eg, investors might be afraid to own stocks after a crash). A company could also require the funds within a specific time frame (quick!) and this could alter the means of capital raising the company decides to pursue.
- **Financial costs:** For borrowing, a company would compare the different interest rates on a loan versus bond issue as well as stipulations regarding posting collateral or the seniority of the loan. For selling ownership stakes, the price is a natural concern. In both cases, transaction fees (eg, bank and legal fees) and tax implications would also be considered.
- **Administrative costs:** These primarily stem from filings that the regulatory bodies (eg, the SEC or FSA) require for selling securities (stocks, bonds, etc) to the public. For example, listing stocks on US exchanges generally requires companies to compile several audited financial statements every quarter. This requires much time and effort and also creates transparency that may help out or create competition.
- **Emergency funding/survival:** An unexpected liability surfaces or the core business is sinking and the company scrambles to keep it afloat.
- **Control:** This refers to the notion that many private equity investors/firms demand terms of managerial influence so they can have a say in how the company is run. The other side of this coin would be an IPO in which the company is then ultimately governed by the shareholders via a board and voting system.

Given all of the different reasons companies need to raise capital, the many different types of financing available, and multiple considerations to take into account, CEOs and CFOs will often rely on the advice of their investment bankers.

In the case of a corporation issuing securities (eg, stocks or bonds) to the public, these are called *primary market* transactions since they company is selling its securities directly to the public. In general, it is not possible for investment bankers to know the inner workings of each market segment (eg, stocks, bonds, convertible bonds, etc). Moreover, being bankers with a corporate clientele, neither will they know the investors and clients to which the securities will ultimately be sold. As a result, these transactions are generally brought into the bank by the investment banker but then executed by a *capital markets* team.

Capital markets teams are generally broken up by asset class so that they can focus on that asset and related products. The two most common capital markets teams are equity capital markets (ECM) and debt capital markets (DCM) teams, though other areas such as foreign exchange often have dedicated capital markets teams as well. The bulk, if not all, of the capital markets team will sit on or near the trading floor and leverage expertise from the *sales and trading team* (explained in the next section). This allows them to have a deeper understanding and close pulse on the specific underlying markets and related products. They will generally be capable of structuring transactions and recommending different solutions depending upon the corporate client's needs, current market conditions, or investor demand (recall that the investors will be the ones buying the new issues).

In a nutshell, one might think of a capital markets team as sitting between bankers who service corporate (and other) issuers and the sales/trading franchise that services investors who buy such securities (both primary and secondary markets). They are the touch points for investment bankers looking at different solutions for their corporate clients. As such, they also serve as an additional buffer to keep confidential information from leaking into restricted areas such as the sales/trading teams.

Different teams within the capital markets group are often involved at all stages of a deal, whether it is executed or not. From the initial stages, they could either respond to inquiries from bankers investigating potential ideas or they could proactively provide the bankers with ideas stemming from client demand (eg, there are many investors looking to buy a specific kind of security).

The *origination* team is generally responsible for such activities. Once a corporate client looks interested and an idea has gained some momentum, the capital markets team will stay on top of the market conditions and investor demand, keep the banker and his client informed, and propose different structures that might be suitable to the clients needs. This often requires much iteration. Ultimately the *syndication* team would build and manage client demand leading to the actual execution. They would rely heavily on their colleagues in sales who regularly liaise with investors who would buy such securities.

Figure 8: Illustration of Capital Markets Teams Link Investment Banking and Sales & Trading Operations

Investment banking
→ Corporate and government client relationships
→ Origination via client request and research

Capital Markets
→ Pulse on the markets
→ Structuring
→ Syndication
→ Origination via investor demand side

Sales and trading
→ Distribution channel to institutional investors
→ Trading / execution ability
→ Research

2.1.2 Strategic Advisory

Strategic advisory is essentially the more evolved version of what the mergers and acquisitions (M&A) division was historically. M&A has always been a bread and butter business for investment banks. Indeed, investment banks were always eager to rake in fees and help corporations by advising them on mergers and acquisitions. However, this business has evolved into a much broader array of advisory services and the literal translation of the M&A label does not necessarily do justice to the activities of modern day *strategic advisory* (or *advisory* for short) divisions.

History indicates that M&A activity is pretty well correlated to economic activity. Economic booms often lead to spurts of mergers and acquisitions but business generally slows down when the economy slows down. Below we list some of the peak periods in M&A activity and briefly describe the factors that were involved:

Figure 9: Peaks of M&A Activity

Period	Motivating factors	Why did it end?
Late 19th century	→ Industrial revolution and technological progress → Virtually non-existent anti-trust laws	→ Failure of M&A to achieve the intended synergies → Recession and early 19th century stock market crash
Post WWI	→ Vertical rather than horizontal mergers → Lax margin requirements	→ Depression and stock market crash → Liquidity dried up
Late 1960s	→ Booming economy and stock market → Financial trickery	→ Poor results → Government clampdown → Exposed financial manipulation
1980s (probably the all-time peak with so many mega-mergers)	→ Economic expansion → Deregulation → Leverage	→ War and economic slowdown → Many abuses exposed (eg. Milken) → Government clampdown
Post Gulf War 1990s	→ Globalization → Growing economy → Buoyant market and dot-com mania	→ Economic slowdown → Tech bubble popped and many investors burned

While Figure 9 above gives some insights as to the drivers of M&A activity, it also indicates that there are long periods in which M&A activity is relatively muted. Accordingly, investment banks have expanded their offerings to include a broader array of services, many of which can be productive with or without economic tail winds. Markets have expanded and transactions have become increasingly complex, thus prompting banks to evolve accordingly. No matter the cause, most large investment banks have significant divisions dedicated to a broad array of advisory services which we have dubbed *strategic advisory*. We summarize some of these key advisory services below. It is worth noting that many of these services overlap with the work and advice that bankers in capital raising divisions provide. As a result, efforts are sometimes collaborative while at other times they are competitive.

Mergers and acquisitions: This is a bread and butter business for most investment banks. Bankers will advise clients on potential opportunities to merge with or acquire other businesses. They will also guide companies as to how they can defend themselves against takeovers (ie, takeover protection). Mergers and acquisitions generally come in two flavors: vertical or horizontal. Vertical transactions generally involve a company acquiring either its service providers, suppliers or distributors in order to integrate most of the business starting with product creation all the way through to reaching the final customer. Horizontal transactions refer to those where a company is expanding but via new business areas. This type of activity is what creates conglomerates that house many different types of businesses or companies.

Internal mergers: There are often opportunities within companies whereby they can combine different business units to create synergies. Large companies, especially those that have acquired or merged with others, often end up with redundant activities in different divisions. Merging such areas can reduce the number of redundant efforts, thus improving efficiency.

Spin-offs: Internal businesses that are essentially independent of the broader company it sits within are sometimes sold off. There can be several different motivations for spin-offs. For example, the holding company may simply want to raise cash or streamline its operations. Or some business units might be undervalued on the balance sheet simply due to historical accounting rules that do not accurately assess their value. As a result, a company might choose to sell partial ownership of the business in order to get a new (and hopefully higher) market based valuation of the business.

Divestitures: Following the literal definition, this is where companies completely rid themselves of specific assets and/or businesses. They will no longer exist on their balance sheet or contribute to the income statement. This could be in the context of streamlining or simply disposing of poor performing businesses or unwanted assets.

Restructuring: This term can have broad implications, possibly spanning any/all of the previous three areas discussed above. Here we refer to restructuring in the context of distressed or insolvent companies. Such companies may need to restructure themselves in order to survive. For example, existing or new creditors may want the company to pledge specific assets or businesses as collateral and they may need to restructure in order to do so. This could entail selling off assets or businesses as above, but it might also require isolating (demerging) or merging businesses, cash flows, or assets. It is worth noting that these strategies can also apply to healthy companies as well, but the term restructuring is often associated with distressed companies.

Valuation: Companies often own assets or businesses that they do not know how to accurately assess. These could be ones they own or are interested in purchasing. Even if they do not intend on buying or selling them, they may need some figures for their own accounting. Bankers can perform in depth analysis. This can be a discounted cash flow analysis or they can also compare the business units to other similar businesses that are publicly traded and thus have valuations (stock prices).

Risk management: Corporate clients, including banks, must balance risk and reward for each business or project in which they are involved. They must also assess their overall financial risk as well. Bankers can help out in this area by looking at each unit on its own, but also put together a comprehensive picture of the risks that could impact the firm on a larger scale. Risk is naturally a broad topic spanning many areas, but some examples might include:

– Market based risks such as exchange rates for multinational companies
– Potential regulatory or political risks that could impact specific business units
– Asset liability management
– Credit scoring for lenders
– Assessing various insurance and re-insurance solutions

Capital raising: While some of this advice will come from bankers in the capital raising division, companies looking to raise capital often seek advice from various sources. These companies may be looking for more potential solutions or just want some impartial advice. The transactions could range from relatively simple to highly complex transactions that require much structuring with financial, accounting, legal and other implications (eg, a leveraged buy-out).

2.2 Sales and Trading

Caveat: Given that most of my experience has been working within equity/equity derivatives businesses, the following content tends to be biased towards this area (especially examples). That being said, the concepts and examples generally apply to all other asset classes as well.

The first section here explains how these businesses fit within the broader firm and how they are organized themselves. The next section explains the core business model for these businesses, how they make and lose money. The third section expands on this and explains the other components which augment the core model and makeup what is the most common structure for sales and trading businesses across most major investment banks. The last section discusses some of the politics and incentive structures that can play a significant role in how the business operates and how people are rewarded.

2.2.1 Organizational Structure

Within a bank, sales and trading businesses are generally divided into their separate asset classes. So there would be an individual sales and trading division for equities, bonds, foreign exchange, etc. Each business line focuses on dealing in its own securities, though there can be some overlap. For example, a convertible bond is a bond which can be *converted* into an equity security (ie, a stock). It is what is commonly referred to as a hybrid security, bearing features of more than one asset class. As a result, convertible bond businesses could be placed within the bond or equity business, or perhaps on its own.

Within each asset class, there is a further breakdown between *cash* and *derivatives* units. Figure 10 below illustrates this structure. When we use the word *cash* in this context, we are referring to the *spot* markets. These are markets such as equities (stocks) where the securities are paid for in cash, on the spot; payment and delivery occur immediately after the transaction is agreed[12]. The derivatives we refer to here are financial, not mathematical derivatives. In a nutshell, one can think of a (financial) derivative as a contract between two parties whereby each party agrees to a payout between each other that is *derived* from one more underlying securities. As there are hoards of

---

12   Actually, it generally takes multiple days for the cash and the security to reach each other's account after a transaction has been agreed. The convention they use to describe the maximum number of days allowed is T+N where T represents the transaction date and N the number of days after.

websites and books dedicated to this topic, we only include a brief description of what we believe to be the most common derivatives in Appendix B: Four Very Common Derivatives.

Figure 10: Generic Sales and Trading Organizational Structure

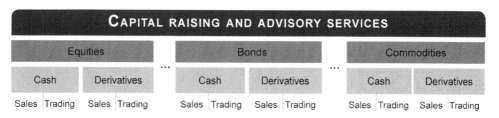

Another distinction that is made, both in cash and derivatives markets, is between *listed* and *over-the-counter* (OTC) markets. While not always the case, this distinction can sometimes lead to an additional organizational barrier or split. Put simply, listed markets are those in which the securities are traded via exchanges (as described in Chapter 1). OTC market transactions are between buyers and sellers; there is no exchange in the middle to intermediate counterparty risk. In the end, an OTC trade is essentially a contractual agreement between you and your counterparty. Even though OTC markets are regulated in order to help protect investors, you still have the risk of them defaulting. The ISDA (International Swaps and Derivatives Association) actively works to mitigate this risk in the OTC derivatives market. They focus on documentation, collateral, legal, and other issues where they can promote sound practice and risk management.

Counterparty risk aside, arguments can be made for both listed and OTC trading. Transparency, fees, and flexibility are three major factors. Exchanges publish their transactions as quickly as possible, thereby enhancing transparency. It is worth noting, however, that some parties prefer not to disclose their transactions. Two clear downsides to listed trading are that exchanges charge fees for their services and their flexibility is limited. OTC trading products can be customized to accommodate specific needs and generally do not have transaction fees like listed products.

A distinction that is made between most roles but generally never explicitly shows up in an official organizational chart is the classification between *front, middle or back office* roles. These labels are attached to all of the positions that are related to the sales and trading businesses. They are also used in different areas of investment banks and other institutions, though perhaps to a slightly lesser extent. These labels are based on one single factor: How directly does the job contribute to revenue generation of the firm? For example, a trader who manages a book (ie, is responsible for a profit or loss account via buying and selling securities) directly contributes to the bottom line of a business, as does a sales person who brings in large deals from which the bank profits. However, an IT consultant who helped program the risk management system used by the traders does not contribute directly to the P&L of that business.

Roles that contribute to the P&L directly (eg, trading and sales) are often labeled *front office roles*. Roles that support a business but do not directly impact P&L (eg, IT and risk monitoring) are labeled as *back office roles*. In recent years the *middle office* classification has emerged and taken on an identity of its own. As the name implies, these roles fall somewhere in between front and back office. The middle office label broadly refers to staff that directly support and work with the front office on a regular basis. Some of them sit on the trading floor while others sit with the rest of the back office.

These classifications can be fuzzy in different contexts. Research, for example, often does not generate revenue directly. But it is also instrumental to the business strategy for many firms. As such, research is often classified as front office despite it often being technically classified as a cost center (any group that does not generate revenues is a cost center).

2.2.2 Core Business Model

As we discussed in Chapter 1, investors can buy and sell various securities via banks or brokers once they are public (ie, after an IPO or debt issue). These are called *secondary markets* (recall that the initial transaction whereby the corporation sold the securities to the public is said to take place in the *primary markets*). In order to facilitate liquidity (ie, the ease with which investors can buy and sell), banks will *make markets* in most of the biggest stock and bond securities. In other words, they will agree to provide bid and ask prices for those securities so that their clients will always have a place to buy/sell the securities.

If a client wants to transact in a specific security, he can request a market and the bank will provide two prices: one at which the bank will buy (their *bid*) and the other at which they sell (their *ask* or *offer* price). Naturally, the bid price will be lower than the ask price or the client would be able to buy and sell for a riskless profit. Once the client decides to buy or sell, the bank's trader will end up with a new position. If the client sells, the bank will then own the stock. If the client buys, then the bank will be short[13] the stock.

An example may help clarify the essence of this business. Consider a bank that makes a market of $99-101 for stock ABC. That is, investors can either buy shares of ABC for $101 or they can sell them for $99. If an investor does indeed come along and sell 1,000 ABC shares (for $99), the bank will pay the investors and then own these shares. The bank generally prefers not to have any such positions since the value of the shares can fluctuate significantly. The bank would prefer for another investor to come along and buy (for $101) so that they could then book a quick profit of $2,000 (buy 1,000 shares for $99 and sell them for $101). In order to encourage a buyer to come along, the trader might even change his market (ie, bid and ask price levels) to reflect his preference to sell his shares. He could offer the shares at a lower price and make a market of say $98/100. These lower prices will encourage buying and discourage selling. If another buyer does like the lower price and comes along and buys his 1,000 shares, the trader will be able to book a profit of $1,000. However, if another seller comes along, the trader may end up buying more shares, albeit at the lower price of $98, thus lowering the average price he has paid for his holding. In this case, he will own more shares of the stock and be more vulnerable to market swings. Accordingly, the trader will have to use his expertise to manage this risk. He could readjust his markets or he could take other positions to offset these risks. Balancing these risks and producing a steady stream of profit is a sign of a good trader.

We made an assumption in the preceding example: clients would come to the trader with their buy and sell orders. In order to profit from market-making, traders need clients to come to them with their buy and sell orders. They are essentially profiting from the bid-ask spread, attempting to buy low and sell high. This is where the sales force comes into play. It is their job to maintain relationships with numerous clients and solicit those clients' orders.

---

13   We describe the concept of shorting in the appendix, but the reader can assume that being short is simply the opposite of being long (ie, owning) the shares so that they profit if the shares go down in price but suffer a loss if the shares rise.

For large banks, these clients are primarily institutional (think of institutional clients as mutual funds, pensions, and other large clients who buy and sell in large quantities). There are also specialized sales teams who service corporations as clients when they need to buy or sell securities. Given that knowledge of corporate transactions amounts to insider information, this business is done "over the wall". Those involved in the transaction with a corporate client are not allowed to deal in or liaise with those dealing in its securities (sales, trading, research) until some specified period after the transaction is completed or withdrawn.

We describe these institutional clients in more detail in the next chapter but there are two primary reasons banks focus on institutional clients and specifically exclude retail business (ie, business from individual investors). First, retail business would require too much time and resource to be profitable. The client / trader ratio would be much too high for any trader to effectively manage. This is the reason why banks and brokerages setup retail brokerage operations; they are built for high frequency, low margin business. The other reason investment banks do not detail with retail clients is that they are not allowed. Allowing a bank to trade directly with average Joe's off of the street is akin to letting a professional poker player into your home game. There is simply too much liability in that retail clients could easily be or appear to be taken advantage of.

So the role of a sales force is to create *order flow*. In general, more order flow helps the market-makers (ie, the traders) capture more bid-ask spread and make more money. It also helps them get a pulse on what investors are doing (buying or selling) with different securities, which can give them an edge. Trading businesses where there are higher volumes and a higher frequency of orders are called *flow* businesses since they are based on a stable stream of customer order flow. This applies to both cash and derivatives markets.

Some banks deal in securities or products that trade less frequently. In other words, they are less liquid than flow products. The dealers know in advance that once they buy or sell these less liquid products, they will likely not be able to flip them out quickly as with flow products. Instead, they will have to figure out ways to manage the risks that those products expose them to and hedge[14] accordingly. Depending upon the type of product, this could require as little as

---

14   Hedging is the process of reducing risk.

a few days to manage or it could take many years. At the extreme, some positions might be too difficult or prohibitively expensive to hedge and traders may choose (or be forced) to sit with the position on their books unhedged.

While not necessarily in the spirit of market making, some trading businesses also employ *proprietary traders*. These traders risk the firm's capital to speculate on markets and securities, usually, but not always, focusing on the asset class within which they sit. They are essentially an internal hedge fund (we describe hedge funds in more detail in the next chapter). As such, they should not be privy to sensitive information about client trading activities. There should be a Chinese wall between them and the market-makers, though they will have access to the same trading tools and public research as other traders.

2.2.3 Complete Business Model

The previous section describes only the core business of a sales and trading business. Few if any of the large investment banks run their businesses with just those two components. Here we describe a more complete model, one that most investment banks use. In particular, we discuss four additional groups that work together with sales and trading to enhance the core business model: research, structuring, analytics, and risk management.

The actual mandates of research teams vary from bank to bank and amongst the divisions within, but the core purpose of research is to facilitate more business for the firm. Here we focus on the sales and trading business, but investment bankers also utilize the research team's[15] expertise since the research analysts' insights can be very useful when analyzing potential and active M&A deals.

Research divisions attract and retain clients by providing them with useful data, insightful commentaries and profitable trade ideas. The goal is to build clients' dependency on the research product and make them feel more indebted so that they reward the firm with more business. In addition to actual published research, clients will have varying degrees of access to research analysts, data, and tools.

Research teams also target polls, surveys and awards to raise their profile. Clients naturally do not want to miss out on any good recommendations and

---

15   Here we refer primarily to equity and credit analysts.

or not be in the know. Accordingly, more impressive research can result in more business from clients.

> **Quick comment:** Savvy clients often spread out their business amongst different banks in order to maintain access to research and tools from multiple sources.

A research department will often include an *index group*[16]. This group will create and maintain proprietary indices which serve as benchmarks for different assets, regions, sectors, or other factors. The primary goal is to promote the indices and then charge other parties (clients, competitors, etc) for using those indices or related data. MSCI (Morgan Stanley Capital International) is a good example since they have been creating and maintaining a wide variety of equity indices for over 40 years.

The next group that also helps sales and trading businesses make more money is *structuring*. This group creates structured products and solutions to sell to clients. In this context, the word *structured* is essentially synonymous with *customized*. There is no universal delineation between what is structured or not structured. We can broadly define structured products as those which cannot be replicated by a static combination of existing products (including vanilla derivatives). However, it is often the case that they will *structure* a product around a current theme or idea that their research department is pushing, even if the product itself is vanilla in structure.

One structured product that has been very popular for decades is CPPI (constant proportion portfolio insurance). In a nutshell, this is a rules based product which increases or decreases exposures to risky assets (eg, equities) based on a floor portfolio (or maximum sustainable loss) parameter chosen by the investor and guaranteed by the bank. As markets rally, the product increases its holdings of risky assets; as markets sell off it decreases its exposure to ensure the portfolio's value does not breach the specified floor or loss limit. Despite the popularity, there is strong criticism against CPPI. One argument is that CPPI buys high as markets rise and sells low as markets fall. But the most significant concern is that these products exacerbate market volatility as they add to the selling or buying when markets are already moving. They

---

16   We discuss the concept of indices and benchmarks in the next chapter.

are often cited as the main driver of Black Monday (a severe market crash on October 19, 1987).

Another example of a structured product pays a client a return based on the best performing asset from a pre-specified basket at expiry. There have been many such products based on "*best of*" and "*worst of*" payouts that have been sold in recent years. These products cannot be replicated via the underlying assets or vanilla options on them. The product actually involves an element of correlation that cannot easily be hedged. These products are just one simple example of the innovation and financial engineering that has created a broad spectrum products based on creative payoff profiles.

In the years before the credit crisis, there was a huge push to structure products to compete with other investments. While they had always targeted institutional investors such as pensions and insurance companies, these clients were generally conservative in their approach to investing and skeptical about *structured* products[17]. However, there was another clientele that was growing quickly and willing to invest in these products: private banks[18] (primarily in Europe and Asia). This emerging clientele was becoming a major source of revenues for banks and they built businesses around them: dedicated sales units, dedicated structuring teams, etc.

Given the complexity of structured products, they often require dedicated trading desks that are well versed in managing different strains of risk. These are generally called *exotic trading* desks and are usually extensions of the flow derivatives desks. Whereas the flow traders are generally divided amongst specific sectors with which they are very familiar, exotics traders are generalists in that they deal in all sectors. They can always check with the flow trader to see if there is anything they should know about a given company or asset they are trading. Their expertise and focus is more on pricing and hedging more complex products. This leads us to our next and third group that supports this type of business.

---

17   Institutional investors were not sufficiently skeptical about some structured products, namely CDOs (collateralized debt obligations). Once CDOs were endowed with an investment grade rating, investors readily invested in these highly structured products that eventually led to great losses. See the appendix for more details.

18   Private banks are essentially financial services firms for wealthy people and families. We describe them in the next chapter.

In order for banks to deal in derivative products, their traders need tools to price and hedge these complex instruments. Before transacting a derivative product, a trader needs to figure out what the price should be. After transacting, the trader will need to identify what their risks are and how to hedge them. Most banks employ highly quantitative groups called *derivatives research*, *analytics*, or *quantitative analytics* devoted to building tools to serve these purposes.

At the heart of these derivative modeling tools is the Black-Scholes pricing framework. As helpful as this model has been and as much as it has changed the industry, there have been and continue to be many developments in this field. Given the heavy modeling involved, most people in these teams possess PhDs from a technical field (eg, mathematics, physics, etc). And due to the commonality of the modeling and mathematical finance issues across asset classes, these teams are usually centralized and run as a single unit, though divided into teams that focus on specific asset classes. We discuss this group in more detail in Chapter 5.

The fourth and last group is *risk management*. There are many types of risk that can threaten the well being of a business. The primary mandate of risk management is to develop and implement strategies to monitor and mitigate many types of risks. Three primary areas of risk are market, credit, and operational risk.

Market risk stems from positions banks have in different securities and derivatives; these positions go up or down in value as the market moves. Risk management will work with trading management to designate specific measurements to monitor different risks. These will include exposures to equities, interest rates, and other asset classes as well as derivatives exposures. Risk management teams will design and use systems to track these quantities as close to real-time as possible.

These risks exist at different levels (eg, trader, department, firm level). As such, they are analyzed and aggregated to assess overall risk to the firm. At the most granular level, most banks will ensure that each trader's risks are monitored separately as to identify anyone who might be taking excessive risk relative to their mandate. Each trader and trading unit is given trading limits that they are not allowed to violate without getting specific permission. These risks are then aggregated to summarize risks for larger sections and ultimately the entire business for a holistic view of its risks.[19]

Quick comment: Most traders' compensation levels are correlated to how much profit they make for the bank through their trading activities. If they make huge profits for the bank, they will likely receive enormous bonuses. However, if they make huge losses, at worst they will lose their job. As a result, their risk profile is asymmetric and may encourage them to take ever larger risks, even if they are not prudent. This profile whereby traders have significant upside *risks*, but minimal downside risk, is similar to that of a call option[19] and thus makes risk management that much more important.

While this process naturally requires summing up exposures across each asset class, they will also attempt to identify *concentration* risks (sometimes called *specific* risks) that might arise. For example, the equities trading unit may have significant exposures to the XYZ company, but still within their risk limits. However, the corporate bond desk might also have significant exposures to the bonds of XYZ, which again do not pose too much risk on a standalone basis. When viewed together, risk management may decide that they have too much risk concentrated in the XYZ company. If it were to fail, its share price and bonds would both collapse. Accordingly, it is important for them to monitor these types of risks that could otherwise go unrecognized.

Credit risk is another significant area which requires monitoring. Credit risk is effectively any exposure the bank has to its counterparties not paying them money owed. The most straightforward example would probably be a direct loan. However, banks also take credit risk when the deal with their clients via other transactions. For example, a client could enter into an OTC derivative position with the bank. If the position goes against the client, they will owe the bank money. Even if they do not owe money at inception, the bank does have exposure to the risk of not being paid by its clients.

---

19   See Appendix B: Four Very Common Derivatives for a description of a call option.

Just as with market risk, credit risk is aggregated in different ways. They attempt to monitor the firm's exposure to specific clients, types of clients, sectors, regions, etc. They do not want to be too exposed to any one factor and therefore actively work to diversify their risks. For example, the growth of the hedge fund business has grown significantly in recent years. This has created concern for this type of client as their strategies are often leveraged and prone to more risk than most other institutional clients. Credit risk departments monitor this sector closely and impose strict guidelines for dealing with these clients.

Operational risk is very different from market and credit risk. Intuitively, one might think of operational risk as anything that could significantly threaten the continuity and well being of the firm's businesses. This could involve computers, people, or external events. Some examples might be computer crashes, employees or clients involved in fraud, or even the impacts from severe weather on personnel and/or systems. The operational risk team will create systems and procedures to monitor and mitigate these risks.

No discussion of risk management would be complete without mentioning the concept of *value at risk* (VaR). Indeed, most every bank (and business line) is required to report VaR figures as a part of their risk management efforts (it is often a regulatory requirement). As the name implies, this figure indicates *how much value is at risk*. The figure is specific to a time horizon and probability (often 5%). Mathematically, V@R indicates the amount of loss of which there is only a 5% chance of being worse; it is the 5th percentile of a portfolio's loss distribution.

While V@R is widely used, it has some inherent flaws. The two largest flaws are probably [1] the fact that asset and business values do not conform to statistical distributions (eg, the *normal* distribution) and [2] different assets and businesses have varying degrees of correlations. Accordingly, V@R figures can at best only be approximations in practice. Nevertheless, they can be helpful and banks use them for many different purposes.

Figure 11:Generic Illustration of an Equity Business Platform

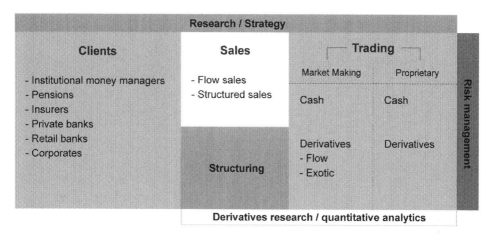

Figure 11: Generic Illustration of an Equity Business Platform above depicts an example of an equity trading business. The generic structure and its components would be similar for other asset classes (eg, fixed income, foreign exchange, commodities, etc). The illustration is not meant to be a physical layout, but adjacent areas are meant to indicate that those units have regular interaction. The structure of the platform will largely depend on the client base and product offering.

2.2.4 Politics and Miscellaneous Concerns

In describing the individual components and their roles in the broader business, we passed over a few critical issues relating to the dynamics between the groups and how revenues are attributed amongst them. In this business it is very important to keep track of who produces the revenues; otherwise, everyone would stand up and say they were responsible for the profits and therefore deserve the lion's share of the bonus pool.

Even traders who have specific profit or loss figures attached to them cannot claim that they are entirely responsible for those figures. The sales force, whose clients' transactions were instrumental to this process, will also claim credit for some of those profits (rarely if ever will they claim credit for losses!). In order to keep track of sales persons' contributions, most firms operate a system of *sales credits*[20]. For each transaction that a salesperson brings

---

20   These go by different names, but *sales credits* seems to be the most common. Most other names hint at the value client transactions bring to the firm (eg, *client value added*).

and executes, they will effectively assign themselves a sales credit for a share of the estimated profit.

Consider a situation where the bank is making a market of $99/101 on a security and a client buys at 101. In theory, the real value of the security would be approximately $100 (the average of $99 and $101). So the trader has made a *paper profit*[21] of $1 (half of the bid-ask spread). Given that the sales person brought the trader the transaction, the sales person could claim credit for a share (eg, half) of that $1 paper profit.

Different trades get rewarded with different levels of sales credits. Some trades are riskier than others and will actually cost the trader money to manage. Other trades are easier to manage or unwind. Traders love it when the sales force brings both a buyer and seller for a transaction so he does not have to manage any residual position.

As a result of this system, even when a trader has a profit booked to his account, a significant portion of it may be credited to others. Sometimes a trader owes more in sales credits than he has in profit. In this case, management will have to find out whether the trader has not been managing his risk properly (starting with his prices) or if sales has been bringing transactions that are difficult to extract profits from. It is not unheard of for a sales person to try and book sales credits regardless of whether the associated transactions actually make money for the firm.

Some structuring teams also use a similar system, booking sales credits for transactions that are based on products they create. However, as the sales force is still ultimately responsible for bringing the client who transacts, sales credits are sometimes split or layered to account for both claims. It often depends on how the different units (sales, trading, structuring) are setup.

It might seem intuitive for research to follow a similar model where they would claim credit for transactions that they recommended. However, there is a potential conflict of interest that can evolve when research is not independent from the trading business. For example, much of the research written

---

21   A paper profit or loss occurs when a trader has bought (or sold) something and its value has changed. He has not yet sold it and realized the profit or loss.

during the dot-com bubble was deemed to be intentionally misleading. Some very high profile research analysts were writing recommendations which they did not actually believe in (often they believed the opposite!) simply to help the firm generate profits.

As a result of these findings, many regulations were passed in an attempt to stop this behavior and ensure the impartiality of research. These regulations were driven by the now infamous Elliot Spitzer who was attorney general at the time. Despite all of this, research management will do its best to get revenue attributed to itself in one form or another. *Soft dollar* arrangements have been used historically, but the essential goal is to lay claim to part of the (potentially higher) commission rates under the assertion that clients are paying extra in order to receive research. It is worth noting that some research units (eg, economics) do not target any specific asset class and therefore cannot follow such a model. However, knowing that their research is used by a broader group of clients (external and internal), these research groups will have to make more subjective arguments to evidence their contributions to the firm.

There is also a balance of power that is different in every firm. The groups that produce the most money generally carry the most sway. In most organizations, this is the trading unit since they are the ones who ultimately book the profits which should exceed the sales credits. However, in some firms it is sales management that calls the shots; the goal of the firm is to generate sales commissions, not P&L. In this environment, the trader's job is to help the sales force book trades and commissions on client transactions, not necessarily trade to generate his own profits.

It is often the case that a desk or unit becomes very successful (profitable) and ultimately wants to break off to form its own standalone business. While the unit that contains the business originally may be reluctant to give up a profitable unit, management will generally not want to risk losing the profitable unit entirely and will spin it off into its own autonomous business. This was likely the case with credit structuring. Many of these teams probably started as a part of a larger desk, but as their own businesses started to generate significant portions of the revenue stream, many eventually spun off to create their own enterprise. We discuss this phenomenon in *Appendix C: The Collateralized Debt Obligation (CDO)*.

2.3 Brokerage

In the previous section we were describing a business in which the banks were transacting directly with clients. In particular, each time the client transacted, the bank would be on the other side of the transaction. In this context, banks are said to be acting as *principals* and are often called *dealers* since they are dealing directly in those securities.

When we use the terms *brokerage* and *broker* we are referring to the business of executing clients' orders and related services (eg, reporting their transactions and account holdings), not taking the other side as principal. Firms which provide execution services in this manner are said to be acting as *agents*. While we use these terms in the strictest sense, it is not uncommon for people to label anybody involved in the markets as brokers or dealers.

The following is divided into two sections. Just as with our description of the sales and trading business, we first describe the traditional core services that brokerages offer their clients and then expand on that, explaining the broader spectrum of services that brokerages have evolved to offer.

2.3.1 Core Services

An intuitive way to think of a brokerage is as an interface to the markets. For example, if Joe Investor off the street wants to buy a stock on the New York Stock Exchange (NYSE), he cannot simply stroll into the NYSE building and do so. In fact, he cannot even open an account there. Exchanges only allow their members to execute trades with them. Recall from Chapter 1 that one of the primary functions of exchanges is to mitigate risk by intermediating transactions. Accordingly, exchanges must maintain strict requirements for their members who they deal with.

So what does a broker do with an order? In general, a broker can either execute trades electronically or over the phone. Orders placed electronically can get routed either directly to the exchange or into an electronic trading system which aggregates many market participants buy and sell orders. Orders placed over the phone may be directly to traders on an exchange's trading floor or market makers at another firm. Figure 12 below describes some of the primary types of orders that clients can place with their brokers.

For the benefit of clients who are at the mercy of brokers who execute their orders, regulators impose strict protocols for brokers to follow. Generally speaking, these regulations are geared towards ensuring brokers execute clients' orders in a fair and timely manner. Given that brokers make their money on the commissions they make from executing orders, it is in their best interest to do well by their clients to keep them coming back.

Figure 12: Common Order Types

Market order	Execute the order immediately at whatever price possible. Given that bid and ask prices are only valid for a specified size, larger orders will execute the remainder of the size to the next best bid or offer and so on. This can result in poor execution.
Limit order	Executes an order at a pre-specified level or better. Can result in the order being partially filled or not getting executed at all. Additional stipulations are also possible in that the client can ask for the order to be executed for a minimum size, for example. In the case that the minimum size is the total size, it is an all-or-nothing limit order.
Working order	Execute an order on a best efforts basis, often breaking it up into smaller pieces executed over a long time period. Good for large orders.
Market-on-open (or close)	Often there is an auction process for the open and/or close of trading whereby (limit and market) orders are placed in a pool (which nobody can see) and the opening or closing price is chosen to maximize the number of securities traded.
VWAP / TWAP	Executions are done in a manner so that the average price of the order matches either the volume or time weighted average price of that security executed over a given time period (usually a day). These are also very popular for large orders since they set an objective benchmark, unlike working orders.

Executing trades is only one facet of the services that brokerages offer. Separate from the execution (ie, the agreement of another counterparty to buy or sell), there are other steps the broker must ensure go smoothly in order for each transaction to be completed. First, the broker must confirm the trade. This essentially amounts to getting a confirmation from the other counterparty that they took the other side of the trade. Then the broker makes sure that the appropriate funds are transferred from the buyer to the seller. At the same time, they will also have to ensure that their client releases or receives the securities they sold or purchased. These latter two processes are known as *clearing and settlement*. In general, most of these steps which follow a transaction occur behind the scenes without any problems. In the rare instance where there is a problem, brokers will work to resolve the issue and only bother the client if necessary.

The entity that actually holds a client's funds and securities is called the *custodian*. This can be the same entity as the broker, though most clients execute through multiple brokers but keep their assets with only one or two custodians. The custodian is responsible for maintaining its clients' positions. This could entail managing dividend or interest cash flows, stocks splits or spin-offs, margining, or other asset services.

In addition to executing and ensuring a smooth transaction, brokers provide their clients with details regarding the transactions. This could be as simple as the trade confirmation mentioned above, or they might include further details such as a breakdown of each order, number of shares traded, total cost, average price, time of trade(s), etc. Unrelated to any specific transaction, brokers and custodians will usually provide their clients with regular (eg, daily) statements which detail all of the positions (and any related activities) related to their account(s). These statements might include details such as the original purchase price and date, the accrued profit or loss, etc.

2.3.2 Expanded Services

While we described the essential services brokerages offer in the previous section, this business has expanded enormously in recent years and now offers a much broader variety of services. A major driver of this growth can be attributed to the growth of hedge funds. Their scale and needs have almost single handedly redefined the offerings of the brokerage industry, benefiting other institutional clients other than hedge funds as well.

In the following, we break most of these additional services down into three primary areas: margin, borrow, and risk netting services. We then end by highlighting several other services which evolved in order to help new clients get started. Many of these services (sometimes labeled *incubation* services) go beyond traditional financial services. In effect, the banks are helping to plant and fertilize seeds for new business.

The first additional service is *margining*. Arguably, this could be included amongst the core services since it is so common. Margining is the process whereby banks lend clients money to buy securities. They do not lend them all of the money since clients could walk away from bad trades leaving the losses with the bank. Banks generally require clients to post as much money as would be needed to cover potential losses from the purchased securities. The end result for a client who uses such a service is *leverage*[22]; the client is taking positions that are larger than the amount of capital he contributes. Leverage can be dangerous in that an investor can more easily lose all of his risk capital (ie, the money he posted with the bank). We illustrate this via an example.

Consider an investor who wants to purchase a security for $100 but the bank only requires that he posts $10 and lends him the other $90. Should the security go down by 10%, the investor will lose $10, all of his capital. Though it depends on the volatility of the asset, in most cases the bank would require a higher percentage of the cost to be posted, say 20% (or $20 in this example). In this scenario, should the security go down by 10% in a given day, the bank will lose $10 of the $20 on the position. It will also have time to ask the investor to post enough money to meet his 20% requirement again; this would be an additional $8 (20% of $90 is $18).

The next service we describe is *borrowing and lending of assets*. This service exists for the purpose of allowing investors to profit from securities going down. To speculate on a security going up, one only has to buy that security. However, in order to profit from it going down, the process is a little more involved. This process is called *shorting* a security.

Appendix A: Shorting and Leverage describes this in detail but we present a brief example here to show how it relates to borrowing/lending.

In order to short a security, a client will first have to *borrow* it from someone who has it (and perhaps does not plan to sell it anytime soon). In return for borrowing it, the client will agree to pay some sort of running fee until he returns it. Once he has borrowed the security, he can sell it. If the security goes down, as he had speculated, he can buy it back at a lower price. Or he can buy it back even if it has not gone down, perhaps to cut his losses. But once he has repurchased the security, he can give it back to the original owner he borrowed it from, booking himself a profit or loss in the process.

---

22   Note that the use of the word *leverage* here is analogous to how we used it in Chapter 1 where we said that a company was leveraging itself when it borrowed funds to run its business. It is precisely the same concept.

This process of shorting we just described has two sides. There are clients who want to short and there are other parties who *lend* them the securities to short with. Institutional investors often require both services. For example, hedge funds often wish to short (borrow) different securities whereas mutual funds (who often hold long only positions) like to lend their securities out and earn extra fees for doing so.

Shorting presents a problem to brokers who are managing their clients' margins. Unlike a long position, a short position can have unlimited losses[23]. So how much margin cash should the broker require the client to post? While the theoretical risk may be unlimited for short positions, if they are used in conjunction with long positions then they are generally offsetting and serve to reduce the overall risk of the portfolio[24].

Clients with long and short positions often demand that their brokers *net their risks* which will require them to post less risk capital. This service is known as *risk netting*. Netting risks is not limited to long and short securities, it also applies to derivatives. Exchanges use a similar system to calculate margins from their clients in order to mitigate the risk of defaults. More sophisticated brokerages will be able to net risks across cash securities and derivatives, and perhaps even across asset classes. Given that hedge funds are so active in shorting and derivatives, they are often very dependent on their brokers for risk netting services.

In addition to the risk netting for cash securities and derivative, hedge funds also benefit from *novation*. Novation is simply the process of assigning a trade to a different counterparty. The reason it becomes important is that hedge funds engage in many OTC trades with different counterparties. Often, they

---

23   Indeed, if you a short a security that has no ceiling on its price (a stock or commodity for example), then you are exposed to unlimited losses as there is no bound for the price you may ultimately buy back at.

24   If an investor is only long, they are exposed to the overall market going down. If an investor is short another security (in addition to his long), then that position will benefit when the market goes down, thereby offsetting the losses from the long position. The risks will also offset when the market rises. On balance, the risk of the net position is lower. Note that this assumes the two securities are positively correlated.

will establish a position with one client and unwind it with another. Instead of leaving the two opposite transactions open, their broker will oblige the other counterparties to face each other instead of the client, thus taking the client out of the middle and relieving him of both positions. It may be easier to understand this concept in terms of betting. If you make a bet with one person and the opposite bet with another person, you have made two bets but they cancel each other out. Instead of having to collect from the loser and pay off the winner, you step out and let them settle the bet directly.

While there is no universal definition, brokerages which offer most of these services are generally called *prime brokers*. Depending upon their needs, clients may have multiple prime brokers. This is usually done for one of two reasons. Different prime brokers offer different services and a client may wish to take advantage of some services from various brokers. Another reason they may use multiple prime brokers is to diversify their risks. As the credit crisis illustrated, large banks also have financial risks and diversifying risks amongst them can be prudent.

In addition to the services just described, brokers have evolved to offer some services which do not have any financial affiliation. The goal is to help catalyze more business for themselves. They do so by helping investment funds (primarily hedge funds) get setup. One of the most important means of doing so is introducing new funds to investors (sometimes they invest directly). Banks naturally have strong relationships with a broad array of investors and will not hesitate to make introductions, often holding conferences dedicated to this very purpose. Aside from helping to raise capital from investors, prime brokers can help new funds find office space, equipments, administrative support, etc. The may even offer basic risk management systems. In effect, they try to create an off-the-shelf platform of services so new funds can be up and running in as little time as possible. In short, they will do almost anything they can to incubate new business. And of course once the fund is setup, they will naturally provide all of their typical brokerage services. These are often called *incubation* services.

Different types of banks

Chapter 2 Concepts

- Bank holding companies (Investment banks, commercial banks, investment management, retail bank, etc)
- Investment banking divisions (Corporate finance, sales & trading, and brokerage)
- Ambiguity of the investment banking label
- Capital raising motivations, considerations, and products
- Chinese wall
- Capital markets groups
- Sales & trading business
  - Core business model
  - Related divisions (eg, research, structuring, analytics, etc)
- Front, middle, and back office positions
- Brokerage
  - Core services
  - Expanded offering

Chapter 3:

Overview of the Buy-side

As mentioned in Chapter 1, the term *buy-side* is a broad label which generally describes financial institutions that utilize the different services banks and brokerages offer (eg, brokerage, market making, derivatives, research, etc). In this context, banks and brokerages are labeled as the *sell-side* as they sell their services to the buys-side.

Much of the buy-side comprises for-profit companies whose sole purpose is to take other people's money and invest it on their behalf; they are commonly called *asset managers*. Mutual funds fall into this category. These firms charge their investors fees to invest their money. These fees can appear in many different forms. Figure 13 lists some of the most common types. Given that many of the fees are based on a percentage of assets, it should not be surprising that many of these firms try to obtain as many *assets under management* (AUM) as they can.

There are other institutions that also focus on investing on behalf of others (or for other purposes) but whose goal is more focused on liabilities or wealth management. Pension funds are one such example. While we include these latter institutions within our definition of the buy-side (those who use sell-side services), not everybody does. As one might expect, jobs in these institutions generally pay less than those in the for-profit realm.

The following is divided into four sections. The first section introduces the notion of benchmarks and indices. The purpose of this section is to lay the foundation for understanding and distinguishing different investment styles of the firms described in the next two sections. The last section here presents a generic structure that most buy-side institutions follow and a brief description of the different units within.

Figure 13: Common Types of Asset Management Fees

Front/back-end loads	Fees charged upon entry/exit of a fund. These are mostly assessed as a percentage of assets, but are sometimes absolute. They range from 0-5% in most cases. These types of fees are typical in some mutual funds.
Management	These are running fees and generally assessed as a percentage of assets. While they are quoted as annual rates, they are assessed and debited monthly in most cases. These fees are usually in the 0-2% range, but funds with stellar track records can charge significantly more.
Expenses	These fees are supposed to cover a firm's expenses and are sometimes listed separately from the management fee.
Performance	These are mostly used by hedge funds. Common practice is to take a percentage of profits, usually 20%. Sometimes there is a hurdle rate whereby this percentage is assessed against profits beyond a stated level (eg, 5%) or benchmark (eg, risk-free rate).

3.1 Benchmarks, Indices and Investing

In the old days, well before the internet and before financial information was broadly available, investors essentially had to trust their brokers with their investments. There were hardly any means by which one could judge the performance of his or her own investments. It was not until the end of the 19th century when someone first created a (stock) market index which was intended for use as an indicator of broad market performance.

Charles Dow created the *Dow Jones Industrial Average* in 1896[25] and it is still used today. Whether it was his specific purpose or not, investors could then monitor the relative performance of their own portfolios against this index to gauge how well their investments were performing. It was a perfect yardstick by which to measure their brokers' investment prowess. Dow used a simple average of share prices for his construction, but other methodologies[26] and indices eventually evolved.

---

[25] He also created the Dow Jones Transportation Index 14 years earlier, but this was focused on transportation companies, a very popular sector at the time. Dow started the Wall Street Journal which has endured the test of time as well.

[26] Indices which weight shares by their market capitalization are the most popular types of index constructions but there are arguments for both approaches. Index construction is still a very active area today.

Indices are essentially investment benchmarks. They are constructed so that they are transparent, objective, and not overly complex; they are meant to be easy to follow. Fast forward a century and there are indices for almost every sector and asset class. Indeed, indices have now taken on a life of their own as many investments are structured to perform precisely in line with particular indices. Perhaps the best example is the ETF (exchange traded fund) which we describe in *Appendix D: The Exchange Traded Fund*. Investments such as these that try to track an index are labeled *passive* investments. They serve as a default investment to which we compare other investment styles in the next section.

3.2 Investment Styles

By investment style, we are referring to the methodology by which one constructs a portfolio of securities or investments. We classify investment styles into two broad categories: traditional and alternative. We define the *traditional* investment styles as those which employ long only (ie, no short positions) portfolios of common securities, generally stocks and/or bonds. These are the most common and most accessible investments. *Alternative* investments cover all other types of strategies, including those of hedge funds, for example.

3.2.1 Traditional Investment Styles

As we highlighted above, investments that attempt to follow the performance of an index are called passive investments and we consider this a default approach. In this case, an investment manager does not attempt to use his own expertise in order to try and select investments. Instead, he simply buys the securities that are included in the targeted index and he buys them in the same proportions as they are represented in the index. In other words, he weights the securities the same as they are in the index.

Some investment managers use the index as a core approach but then deviate just slightly by making adjustments to the weights according to their views. In particular, such a manager would reduce the weights (perhaps to zero) of securities that he did not expect to perform well and increase the weights of those he did expect to perform well. He might even include related securities that were not included as members of the index. This strategy is labeled as an *enhanced index* approach.

Another example of an enhanced index strategy that has been popular in recent years is the *130/30* approach. In most 130/30 strategies, there is an underlying index on which the strategy is based but tries to outperform. It starts with the default passive portfolio. Then it uses a model to forecast (or rank) returns for those securities. It reduces holdings of the securities with lower forecasts which amount to 30% of the total portfolio holdings and uses the proceeds to purchase the securities with higher expected returns.

Moving beyond passive and enhanced strategies we now discuss *active* strategies. Active strategies encompass those strategies which rely on analysis or models to select securities. The managers of such funds may or may not acknowledge a relevant benchmark. Some of these funds use in-depth fundamental analysis. They will examine financial statements, industry trends, speak with management, etc. Other funds rely primarily on quantitative tools to screen the markets and look for opportunities. Some funds will use a combination of fundamental and quantitative approaches.

Perhaps the best known example of an investor who uses the fundamental approach is Warren Buffet. He uses his value investing[27] expertise to select securities for Berkshire Hathaway's portfolio. While Buffet's track record is remarkable in its own right, the sad reality is that most active managers underperform their benchmarks. This has been observed time and time again in both academic studies and industry surveys.

3.2.2 Alternative Investments

As mentioned above, alternative investments are essentially any investments other than the standard long only portfolios of stocks or bonds. Investments involving nontraditional assets such as commodities, real estate, and private equity typically qualify as alternative. Likewise, investments that require shorting, leverage or derivatives are too. We discuss several examples of these alternative strategies in the following paragraphs.

One of the most popular types of alternative investment strategies is *long/ short* or *market neutral*. This strategy is primarily an equity based strategy, but it is possible to implement with other assets as well. These types of funds can

---

27   Value investing is essentially an approach that analyzes the fundamentals of companies and finds those which are trading cheap relative to their fundamentals. In short, Buffet's approach tries to identify well managed companies that have a sustainable competitive advantage over other companies. Readers interested in the topic of value investing should consult Bruce Greenwald's book *Value Investing: From Graham to Buffett and Beyond*.

use fundamental analysis, quantitative models[28], or some combination of the two to select securities. The idea is to establish both long and short portfolios whereby the assets in the long portfolio are expected to outperform but be correlated to those in the short portfolio.

For example, if there are several dot-com or tech stocks in the long portfolio that a manager thinks will perform well, there will likely be some from those sectors in the short portfolio as well. The ones in the short portfolio may be chosen specifically or not. The reason for matching these assets is to reduce the risks of as many factors as possible. So if the equity market were to sell off overall, the long/short portfolio would not be as affected since the profits from the shorts compensate losses in the longs. In this example, if the market was fine overall but the tech sector was to sell off significantly, then the same principle would apply since the portfolio has both longs and shorts in that sector.

It is worth noting that the ratio of long to short portfolios is not always 1:1. Some managers only short a small percentage (eg, 10%) relative to the longs. Other funds actually have a larger percentage short than long. These funds are said to have a *short bias*. At the extreme, there are also dedicated short funds which maintain only short positions.

Another alternative strategy that many funds employ is *macro* investing. These managers use their economic expertise to forecast broad market moves instead of targeting specific securities (though they may augment their strategy by selecting specific securities/assets to express their view). Their primary goal is to forecast where equity, corporate bond, interest rate, currency and/ or commodity markets will go and position themselves accordingly. These funds generally sit on positions for weeks or months, sometimes longer, as they wait for various economic and political situations to unravel.

At the other end of the spectrum are high frequency strategies which require no fundamental or economic data. These strategies execute and unwind positions within minutes, seconds, or milliseconds. Such strategies scour the

---

28   *Quant equity* modeling has become very popular in recent years, possibly even too popular. Many funds started to reduce risk and unwind trades in 2008, many of which were quant equity trades. This unwinding led to the underperformance of others' quant equity trades which then led them to unwind their trades. This created a vicious circle which led to a massive underperformance of the strategies in August 2008.

market for temporary liquidity shortages or imbalances between buyers and sellers (as might be observed in the order book[29]) and execute transactions to take advantage of these situations. This strategy is often called *statistical arbitrage* since the indicators that the asset managers look for are not guaranteed to work for every trade, but rather make each trade more probable to be profitable. Given that these strategies often execute 100s, 1000s, or more trades a day, the law of averages should work out.

The last type of alternative strategy we discuss involves derivatives. Banks deal in derivatives with many different clients and often end up aggregating different risks. In recent years, they have used financial engineering and other derivatives to repackage some of these risks into products that look attractive to hedge funds and other clients. This process by which banks offload these risks to hedge funds and other clients is called *risk transfer* or *risk recycling*.

Examples of two such risks that often get recycled in equity derivatives are volatility and correlation[30]. Banks accumulate significant exposures to these risks in the course of selling structured products to the retail market. Because of their complex nature, it is not easy to find existing products to help banks manage these risks. So they repackage and sell them to many existing and new hedge funds that focus specifically on trading volatility and correlation.

Another older but related example of using hedge funds for risk transfer is the convertible bonds market. A convertible bond is essentially a bond that allows an investor to convert it into equity. This affords the investor an *option* which is embedded in the product. As banks issued significant numbers of convertible bonds, hedge funds emerged as eager buyers of these bonds. They specifically used the embedded option as a means to trade volatility. As more hedge funds recognized the profitability of this strategy, many more started implementing it. It became so popular that the hedge funds eventually created more demand than all of the other regular convertible bond investors combined.

3.3 Buy-side Institutions

Recall that buy-side institutions are generally companies that invest money on the behalf of others. In the course of doing so, they utilize many of the services

---

29   An order book is an electronic market making tool which lists multiple buyers' and sellers' bids and offers.

30   These risks are described in more detail within Chapter 5.

that banks and other sell-side institutions (eg, brokers) offer. Below we provide brief descriptions of the most common buy-side institutions.

3.3.1 Mutual Funds

Mutual funds are one of the oldest and largest buy-side institutions. Many people who are not comfortable investing their own money invest in mutual funds. Mutual funds generally have mandates or benchmarks which they strive to match or outperform. Those which attempt to match or follow a benchmark (eg, an index such as the S&P 500) are called passive managers; those which attempt to outperform a benchmark are called active managers[31]. However, some funds do not adhere to any benchmark and strive to maximize absolute returns for their investors. It is worth noting that exchange traded funds (ETFs) have become very popular over the last decade and are becoming the vehicle of choice for passive investing. For more information on ETFs, please see Appendix D: The Exchange Traded Fund (ETF).

3.3.2 Asset Management Firms

While there are many standalone asset managers, investment banks often maintain their own investment/asset management arms, separate from their investment banking activities. Potential conflicts of interest prevent investment banks from being the sole service providers to their investment management arms. Consequently, most of these investment management divisions are considered to be part of the buy-side. Just like mutual funds, these firms offer a variety of different investment funds catering to client needs, spanning different asset classes and investment strategies.

3.3.3 Pension Funds

Many companies and governments offer pension or social security programs. Given that pension funds manage money on behalf of others, money that is critical to their retirement, they must follow strict guidelines which are designed to limit risk and protect the pensioners' assets.

3.3.4 Insurance Companies

Aside from their own pension funds, the core business lines of insurance companies also have investment needs. The premiums that clients pay insurance

---

31   Unfortunately, most active managers underperform their benchmarks after fees are taken into consideration.

companies need to be invested and managed so that they will be able to pay their liabilities once due. Insurance companies also sell their clients other financial products that embed risks which are based on the market's performance. As a result, they must make investments to hedge these liabilities.

3.3.5 Family Offices

Many wealthy individuals and families maintain investment groups that are dedicated to preserving or growing their wealth. Most of these institutions might not have the economy of scale to directly invest in securities. Instead, they will generally determine an investment strategy and then allocate money to different third party institutions in order to achieve their goals.

3.3.6 Endowments

Many institutions, such as universities and hospitals, setup funds to help manage their assets. Endowments generally get funds in one of two ways; either the institution it serves manages to generate some surplus profits or people loyal to the institution, or its cause, donate money. Historically, endowments have been quite conservative in their investment strategies. But there has been a trend in recent years whereby they increasingly invest in alternative strategies.

3.3.7 Hedge Funds

These are investment firms which manage money using sophisticated investment strategies, most of which fall into the alternative investment category. They can speculate on the long or short side and are able to employ leverage. There are many different types of hedge funds, too many to describe here. Some speculate on macroeconomic events and their impact on different asset classes. Some perform in depth research on individual companies or special situations (eg, mergers) to look for potential arbitrage opportunities. Others employ mathematical algorithms and execute 1000s of transactions a day. In most cases, hedge funds do not attempt to follow a benchmark but instead try to achieve low risk (hence the term "hedge" in their name) and absolute returns. Notwithstanding, many hedges funds, large and small, have taken excessive risks and blown up (ie, lost much and sometimes all of their investors' money). Accordingly, they are often referred to as *leveraged* funds rather than *hedge* funds.

3.3.8 Fund of Funds (FoFs)

As the name implies, these are funds which pool investors' money and then invest it into other funds (primarily hedge funds). Three major factors contributed to the rapid growth of FoFs. First, top hedge funds often imposed high minimum levels of investment which excluded many individual investors from direct investment. FoFs could, however, pool money and access these hedge funds. Second, hedge funds were mostly unregulated and the investing public was largely unfamiliar with their sophisticated strategies. This created a niche for FoFs to fulfill as they performed due diligence to weed out hedge funds whose strategies were not reliable or too risky. Lastly, despite being hedge funds (which are supposed to be hedged), there were still significant risks and FoFs provided a means of diversification for these risks.

3.3.9 Private Equity

These firms invest in private companies, those that are not publicly traded. This includes venture capital but the most popular area within private equity has probably been leveraged buyouts (LBOs). Due to the illiquid nature of private equity investments, investors' money is usually *locked up* for multiple years. In the case of LBOs, they generally buyout public companies with a view of significantly restructuring (eg, sell off assets and business lines, cut down staff, etc) and then selling the newly improved companies afterward. They often employ significant leverage by borrowing most of the money to purchase the company and then hope that the restructured business generates enough cash flow to pay down the debts and emerge as a profitable and attractive investment. It is worth noting that these firms reap huge benefits from the tax relief they get from this leverage (interest is tax deductible) and classifying their profits as capital gains instead of income.

3.4 Generic Structure of Buy-side Institutions

Buy-side institutions are larger in number but smaller in size, on average, relative to sell-side institutions. Accordingly, their size does not allow for an economy of scale in the same way that investment banks often have teams of analysts, researchers, sales, traders, structurers, etc. Those that are not run for profit (eg, pension funds) may have even leaner operations and lower personnel to AUM ratios. There are, however, some very large buy-side institutions that rival in magnitude some of the tier one banks, but it is not the norm.

As a result, many of a buy-side institution's departments are run by a handful of people who may perform multiple roles. There are usually some well defined roles that exist in most firms, even if the personnel who fulfill them are dynamic. We break down and summarize seven such roles that exist within most buy-side institutions in Figure 14 below.

Figure 14: Common Roles Within Buy-side Institutions

Role	Description
Senior management	At the top of for-profit firms are usually the principals, those who have personal stakes in the firm and were around at the firm's inception. They will occupy the senior managerial roles, dictating business strategy and the future direction(s) of the firm.
Asset allocation	This is a senior team responsible for top level asset allocation. That is, they choose how much risk to take, and how much money gets invested in different asset classes (eg, stocks vs bonds) and strategies.
Risk management	Often comprised of high level figures from the above two categories as well as some more junior personnel who aggregate information. The goal for this group is to monitor and mitigate risk wherever possible. In smaller firms, this unit may be a secondary role for several people rather than a dedicated unit.
Portfolio managers (PMs)	Perhaps liaising directly with the asset allocation team, these people have the responsibility of managing specific funds and portfolios. Each fund will have its own mandate and the PM should ensure that it is followed. Making trades themselves and directing others (junior PMs or execution) to make trades is part of the job. They are also responsible for monitoring their portfolios' risks and following up on various administrative tasks that are required to ensure their portfolios are run properly.
Junior PMs	These are essentially aspiring PMs working their way up. Often they will do all of the heavy lifting for the PMs initially. As time passes, they will prove themselves and acquire increased responsibilities such as using their own judgment to make key investment decisions.
Execution	These people are generally professional traders. Their job is not to decide what to buy or sell, but to figure out the best way to do it. They will be familiar with multiple trading systems and have networks of people who they can call on to help them execute trades. They take their orders directly from the PMs.
Research analysts	Often aspiring to be junior PMs, research analysts are there to support PMs in deciding what securities to buy and sell. They will often generate ideas on their own or investigate ideas that different PMs request.
Marketing	For-profit funds will employ marketing teams whose job is to go out and raise capital to be invested in their funds.

Chapter 3 Concepts

- Role of buy-side institutions
- Types of asset management fees
- Benchmarks and indices
- Passive vs active investing
- Traditional and alternative investment styles (long only, long-short, macro, statistical arbitrage, etc)
- Risk recycling
- Buy-side institutions (mutual funds, pensions, hedge funds, etc)
- Buy-side organizational structure

Chapter 4:

Job Descriptions and Compatibility

Hopefully the previous chapters have given you a better understanding of the financial services industry and the functions of various firms and business units within. The purpose of this chapter is to provide you with in depth descriptions for the primary types of roles that exist within the various segments of the financial industry.

For each role, we expand on four topics:

- **Duties and responsibilities –** Describes what skills are required for the role and what the job actually involves on a day to day basis.
- **Career potential –** Discusses how easy (or difficult) it is to maneuver from one role into another. This can be important if you do not land your top choice for a job but still want to angle to get there down the line.
- **Key factors –** Highlights critical factors that are relevant to anyone considering each type of role. These are not necessarily good or bad but may help with assessing compatibility.
- **Pros and cons –** Emphasizes the most important positive and negative features of each role.

Lastly, we conclude this chapter with a scoring system which summarizes each of these roles based on 10 key attributes (eg, earning potential, stress level, required quantitative skills, etc). Our purpose here is to allow one to systematically highlight jobs for which they are well suited and rule out others.

4.1 Highlighting the Primary Roles

We provide overviews of 11 roles. Each falls into one of the four groups below. The first three groups should be familiar from the previous chapters. The fourth is an "other" category. We focus primarily on *junior* roles as these will be most pertinent to readers of this book, though we highlight some more senior roles as potential career options. The order simply follows the order of presentation in the previous chapters.

- **Corporate finance:** We first describe a role in corporate finance (ie, the quintessential investment banker) and then in capital markets which works closer to sales and trading.
- **Sales and trading:** We describe roles in the six primary divisions of sales and trading described in Chapter 2 (sales, trading, research, structuring, analytics, and risk management).
- **Buy-side:** We describe two of the roles that we highlighted in the previous chapter, junior portfolio manager and researcher[32].
- **Other:** Here we describe some other businesses, such as retail and commercial banking, which do not fit into the previous categories. One key distinction is that these businesses leverage a few core products or services and primarily rely on volume to earn money - as opposed to risk taking or deal making.

Corporate Finance

Duties and Responsibilities

One thing that you should acknowledge as a junior banker is that your job is essentially to make others' lives easier by doing as much as the heavy lifting as possible. Needless to say, you should probably do what you are told, even if it involves getting coffees, lunches, arranging meetings, or whatever.

Much of what you might consider actual work will be doing tedious analysis for more senior colleagues; rarely will juniors attend client meetings, let alone contribute. Most of this work will involve Excel. Some of this will be analyzing companies and industries using discounted cash flow and analysis and peer comparison. At times you will have to conduct scenario analyses for potential transactions and the impacts on the involved companies. Much of this analysis will be discarded but some will be input into Powerpoint presentations for senior bankers to present to clients.

A typical day will depend whether or not you are working on a deal that has some momentum or is near closing. If this is the case, your life will be put on hold. That means you will likely be working whatever hours are humanly (not

---

32   While execution and marketing could also be included, that execution is an often commoditized role and thus falls into the fourth category. And marketing is essentially the same as sell-side sales except that the product they sell is different.

necessarily humanely) possible. Evenings and weekends will not exist. At other times, when there are no imminent deals, you could be multi-tasking amongst several different potential deals. Stress levels will come down and you might even have some free time outside of work, though this depends on what kind of bankers you are working for. Notwithstanding, ten perhaps twelve hour days are generally the minimum – even if much of it is face time.

Career Potential

The natural trajectory for junior analysts and associates is upward within the firm but there are some alternative routes. For example, if you are not very good at your job or have incurred the wrath of some senior bankers, your path might cease to exist or perhaps lead to another firm. However, if one is successful at what they do (or can at least convince others of such), then they could move to another firm or over to the corporate side. Or, once one has enough experience, consulting or starting their own boutique investment banking firm are also potential options.

Key Factors

In general, the money is very good, though there is not much pay differentiation between good and poor performers (until the latter is ejected). But you have to be prepared to trade in your free time (evenings and weekends) and give your senior colleagues the right to berate you at anytime whether you deserve it or not. Dealing with enormous egos is certainly a requirement. An office type environment is the norm.

Pros
- Exorbitant pay almost guaranteed
- Exposure to large scale transactions; bird's eye view of corporate finance
- Leads to unparalleled networking; work with senior executives including CEOs and CFOs of major corporations

Cons
- Hours
- Tasks sometime have seemingly impossible deadlines
- Endure senior bankers berating you and your work
- Work can often be more tedious than challenging
- Monetary rewards, while generous, often do not distinguish between good and poor performance

Capital markets[33]

Duties and Responsibilities

Recall that capital markets teams work with investment bankers to generate and execute transactions. Junior capital markets employees can be expected to do a variety of different tasks.

Just like their banker colleagues, their jobs will inevitably involve many tedious administrative tasks (getting coffee, donuts, etc). They will often have to respond to banker or client requests for market color, data, or research. In some cases, they may even be taught how to use some of the firm's tools to price vanilla transactions. But there is one task that is guaranteed to take up large portions of junior capital markets employees' time: putting together pitchbooks.

Pitchbooks are used by bankers and marketers to go around and present ideas and transactions to clients. These pitchbooks will generally consist of two components: content specific to potential transactions and a host of slides devoted to promoting the firm's capabilities and achievements. It is not unheard of for them to bias the ranking criteria to move their firm up the league tables (lists which rank firms based on different criteria). This could be something as simple as measuring by the number of deals versus total size of deals or something more subtle such as including a caveat (perhaps a tiny footnote) indicating the survey only included banks of a particular persuasion based on region or size.

Analysts and associates will be scouring the internet and other resources for data and information to put into pitchbooks. They will go through a seemingly infinite number of iterations trying to get pitchbooks right (as judged by some senior colleague).

Career Potential

Good analysts and associates will be given increased responsibilities that often lead in a particular direction. This could be more advanced pricing, structuring, marketing to clients, etc. Moreover, since capital markets positions get exposed to many different business areas (investment banking, sales, trading, structuring, clients, etc), many alternative trajectories are possible.

---

33   It is worth noting that here we are referring to the capital markets teams that work on primary market transactions. Some people use broader definitions which span all of the sales and trading operations as well.

Key Factors

Just as with corporate finance, money is generally the main attraction and personal free-time is the trade-off. Many of the tasks are time urgent and sometimes require all-nighters. Meritocracy can play a greater role earlier in some positions and potentially accelerate your career. Most positions are within a fast paced trading floor environment.

Pros

- High pay likely especially for quality candidates
- Broad exposure to multiple business lines
- More meritocracy

Cons

- Hours are generally very long and deadlines can be stressful
- Much tedious pitchbook work likely

Sales

Duties and Responsibilities

Sales teams are generally divided between cash and derivatives. Within derivatives, they will split flow and structured products. Not all sales positions are the same nor will they involve the same clients or responsibilities. Working on one desk can be very different than working on another. One critical factor that impacts the type of work done is the frequency and size of transactions. In general, the frequency (size) of transactions is generally highest (lowest) in cash businesses and lowest (highest) in structured products with derivatives between.

The primary goal of sales teams is to generate profitable client transactions for the bank. Starting analysts and associates will get firsthand experience working on the trade floor and seeing how the business operates. They will naturally have to perform a variety of tedious tasks that more senior sales people delegate to them. This could include following up on trades and checking confirmations, working with various middle and back office personnel on administrative issues, bookkeeping, reading and aggregating pertinent research, writing commentaries on market conditions and activity, answering phones, etc. Working on presentations will also be a regular occurrence but not to the extent it is in capital markets.

Sales people generally do not work the same hours as capital markets or corporate finance; twelve hour days are probably the norm, not necessarily the minimum. Moreover, arriving at the office early to prepare for business is necessary. The sales force catches up on news and recent events, often attending a morning meeting at or before seven in the morning. Half to a full hour of preparation is not uncommon.

Career Potential

Sales people often evolve into senior sales people. They generally continue to be a producer or start managing. Producers build up their client base maintain strong relationships which the leverage throughout their career. They effectively keep their sleeves rolled up and grind out more and more transactions from their clients. This naturally has the potential to become monotonous after some time. Successful sales people can also follow a more managerial route wherein they begin to hire other people to broaden their coverage of more clients (producers might also hire one or two people). This can lead to managing large teams to generate transactions and profits. Politics and strategy become more important at more senior levels.

Key Factors

Personal skills are a must for sales roles, though education and aptitude can also help (eg, with derivatives or complex transactions). Getting out of the office to see or wine and dine clients is common; it sometimes involves traveling to other cities or countries. There is definitely fast track potential to exorbitant pay for those who can produce, though your manager(s) will generally take credit for most of your work in the first few years. This is a "do or die" proposition; if you do not produce, you will not last long. The work may not be overly intellectual. Managing high pressure situations and perhaps political strategy at higher level will probably comprise most of the challenge.

Pros

- Very good pay can come quickly and become almost unlimited for strong producers
- Good networking and clientele potential
- Client entertainment perks
- Front line exposure to the mechanics of a sales and trading business

Cons

- Early start and long hours
- Ass kissing (clients and internal)
- Work often more tedious than challenging, sometimes monotonous
- Very political, especially at more senior levels

Trading

<u>Duties and Responsibilities</u>
More than with sales, roles on different trading desks are often entirely different jobs. At one extreme, working on a proprietary trading desk can sometimes be more relaxed, feeling like a mix of trading and research. However, working as a market maker can be entirely different depending upon what is being traded. For example, spot (ie, cash) foreign exchange trading is probably at the other extreme. This can often have the atmosphere of an all day, high speed game of Tetris as traders work to manage tremendous amounts of order flow and news. Most of the other areas, both cash and derivatives, are more balanced.

Junior traders will start learning about trading and risk management systems. They will learn how to book trades into these various systems and liaise with other colleagues in the office to do whatever they can to reduce the workload of more senior traders. This could include trade reconciliations/confirmations, liaising with other colleagues, making/taking phone calls, etc.

Analysts and associates will also have to get lunch for the desk, though this is not driven as much by ego as with investment bankers. Senior traders are managing significant amounts of risk and generally do not want leave their desk and miss anything important.

Days start early so traders can catch up on news and events relevant to what they trade. They must also tie up any loose ends from trades done the previous day. Depending upon the type of trading, the length of the day can vary. Cash traders probably get off earliest, frequently leaving soon after the closing bell. They usually have automated systems to help with processing their trades and managing risk. Derivatives trading and some other areas often require more manual operations. Depending on the products, the systems, and middle/back office efficiency, this can require anywhere from an hour to an entire evening.

<u>Career Potential</u>
Trading can lead to a fast track and seemingly unlimited upside for quality candidates. Trading is very much like sales in terms of career potential; junior traders generally evolve into senior traders either as continued producers or as senior risk managers who manage teams of traders. Producers typically receive increasing amounts of capital to put at risk as their experience proves their abilities. Another option traders, especially proprietary traders, have is to

go to the buy-side. Hedge funds, for example, have been a popular destination for many traders over the last decade.

Key Factors

The money can be amazing for good traders, but success follows the "do or die" mantra. Making money in the market can be very exhilarating, but managing risk and dealing with losses is not for everyone. Remaining objective in periods of duress or euphoria is not a trait everyone shares. Depending upon the desk one works on, the actual work can be intellectually challenging (eg, proprietary trading) or more like a high speed video game that only requires good instincts and fast acting (eg, spot FX trading). In almost all cases though, it will require staring at computer screens for the majority of the day.

Pros
- Very good pay can come quickly and become almost unlimited for strong producers
- Direct ownership of P&L
- Potential intellectual challenges

Cons
- Early start and sometimes long hours required
- Staring at screens
- High stress potential

Research

Duties and Responsibilities

Junior researchers will generally help their colleagues with a variety of differ-ent tasks (getting lunch is usually not one of them). They will mostly acquire data, put it together in a useful format, build spreadsheets, create charts and tables, etc. Most of their work will be targeting publications, presentations, or client requests; however, they also often build tools to automate different tasks or calculations.

Some of the data and information new research analysts may have to find will not be readily available in any one location. Even when the necessary data is found, it often requires some parsing and reformatting to be able to use it. Excel tends to be the primary tool used to work with data, though more quantitative or data intensive tasks sometimes require an analysis software package such as MATLAB, SAS, or S+. Programming is not the norm but may be required for some roles.

While analysts might initially have to focus mostly on data, they will also be required to perform varying amounts of back testing or scenario analysis. Analysts will use historical data to observe how different indicators and assets performed in the past. More quantitative research roles will often develop and test objective trading strategies. These can range from intuitive to black-box in nature depending upon the group.

Career Potential

Research careers can evolve into several other areas. Good researchers with communication skills can usually move up the managerial ranks and eventually run their own team(s). Some decide to move into other areas such as trading or structuring. Others find opportunities on the buy-side as researchers or junior PMs. Still some researchers/teams have been known to start their own independent research firms.

Key Factors

You must be able to work and think independently to work in research. While working with data may be prevalent at the early stages, formulating ideas, in-vestigating them, and presenting them in publications and presentations will be critical as one evolves. In most cases, research presents a good balance of intellectual challenge, work environment, and compensation. You will get great exposure to the business and clients as well. But without question, you will see others making much more money than you, many who are not as smart or perhaps do not appear to work as hard. Notably, researchers have no concrete link to P&L as do traders and sales people. Even if you come up with a trade idea that leads to huge profits, for example, you should not expect to benefit fully as if you were in trading and actually took the risk.

Pros
- Money is generally very good, not great
- Intellectual opportunities abound
- Generally relaxed atmosphere
- Can lead to other good career opportunities

Cons
- Upside to pay is generally limited
- Fast track opportunities rare

Structuring

Duties and Responsibilities

The structuring roles we refer to can vary significantly between banks and even between asset classes within the same bank. For clarity, we are discussing roles within structuring units that are attached to and support other trading units. Some structuring teams (eg, credit/CDO/asset backed) have evolved into their own revenue generating businesses with their own trading facilities.

Junior structurers can work on a variety of different tasks and projects. Many of the tasks will be similar to those in research, working with data and back testing different trading strategies. The goal here will be more to create a new investment product than to simply advise clients. Creating new products requires significant time and effort dedicated to data mining and testing.

Another task that junior structurers generally frequently take on is pricing. This involves complex and often tedious spreadsheets/tools that access the firm's sophisticated pricing and hedging models. It is important for a structurer to know the price of a product/strategy so they can back test it with the costs in mind. However, structurers also tackle many of the simpler (but still structured) pricing requests from clients since the more senior (exotics) traders usually do not have time to respond to them all.

Many structuring roles liaise primarily with the exotic trading desk. They work together to create products that the traders are happy with. The traders must be able to at least hedge the products, but in some cases, a product will actually complement the risks of the trading book. It is up to the structurer to balance these preferences with those of client demands.

Career Potential

Junior structurers can naturally become more senior structurers, sometimes managing their own teams. Good structurers who work well with the trading desk can move into trading. Or those who enjoy the marketing side may be able to move into sales. Some experienced structurers decide to setup their own companies to sell or provide independent consulting advice on structured products.

Key Factors

Money can be very good in structuring since it is usually a revenue generating unit (whether it books P&L or sales credits). The work can be intellectually challenging, but the primary focus is often on creating marketable (not necessarily good or profitable) products. The role and the hours can vary significantly for different structuring units, so it is very important to find out what the unit does and understand exactly what it is that you will be doing.

Pros
- Money can be very good
- Good exposure to the business and product development
- Can lead to other good career opportunities

Cons
- Hours can be burdensome
- Marketability often trumps quality as a goal
- Pricing tasks can be mind numbing

Analytics

Duties and Responsibilities

Analytics groups primarily work with exotic trading desks to create derivatives pricing and hedging models, though they occasionally work with other groups who need quantitative or modeling support. People working in this group are generally labeled as hardcore quants. Analytics groups typically only hire candidates with advanced degrees in quantitative fields.

Much of the work requires significant analysis that is usually done with more advanced quantitative tools and software. Excel and VBA may be used for some simple analysis, but coding skills are essential for the heavy lifting; C++ is probably the most widely used programming language. Most large firms design their own libraries of code and tools for doing much of the work and it is a dynamic toolkit that is continually expanded and refined.

While creating new models may be done by more senior quants, much of the work for beginning associates will revolve around testing and implementing models; though some will also do research to see what types of models are covered in existing literature. Implementing models requires attention to detail and solid coding skills. A misplaced one or zero can lose millions of dollars. Testing new models requires much time and effort devoted to fitting data and calibrating models. These models might be based on closed form solutions, Monte Carlo simulations, tree based models, etc. It is likely that large data sets will be involved (too big for Excel).

Career Potential

Analytic quants usually progress their careers by moving up the ladder within analytics, eventually doing more modeling or managing than coding. These quants work closely with structured product and exotic trading desks and sometimes transition into them, though this was rare in my experience. Analytic quants can also work on the buy-side as more hedge funds attempt to profit from complex derivatives transactions. Some even start their own consulting firms to help with pricing issues that both buy- and sell-side institutions encounter.

Key Factors

These roles are very quantitative and coding is virtually unavoidable. The mathematical nature of the work opens the door to some quirky types (think of your university math professors on caffeine). Grouping a bunch of PhD quants together can produce some interesting behaviors, arrogance is not uncommon. The pay and hours are very good. Some quants operate on an almost nine to five clock, though eight to six is probably more common. The role will often entail liaising with exotic trading and structuring which opens up doors as well. Overall, it is a very good profession for those who would enjoy it.

Pros
- Money can be very good
- Hours are among the best in the industry
- Atmosphere can be relaxed, almost academic
- Can lead to other good career opportunities

Cons
- Quirky colleagues in most analytics teams
- Usually sit apart from the trading floor
- Non-revenue generating group

Risk management

Duties and Responsibilities

Risk management roles can vary widely but there are two major distinctions that help classify roles. The first is whether the role is located in the front office or not. In general, front office roles are for more senior risk managers as space on the trading floor is expensive. The other split is whether a role involves the actual monitoring of risk or devising methodologies to do so. The former comprises 90% or more of all risk management professionals.

Junior risk managers will often solicit (from traders) and aggregate data for more senior colleagues and frequently prepare risk reports. This can involve using internal systems to identify positions and risks, but it also requires direct liaison with traders or other professionals in the business to which they are linked. Most of the work requires basic math and statistical skills and is done in Excel.

Another critical area of risk management is model validation. As discussed, traders and quants build models that they rely on to price and hedge positions. Risk managers are often required to review the models and provide an independent assessment before the model is released. As a result, quantitative backgrounds are often required.

In addition to model validation, risk management also approves new products before they are traded. While market risks are the primary focus, regulatory, operational, reputation, and brand risks are also considered. A bank does not want to tarnish its reputation buy selling toxic products (ie, those which involve potentially enormous risks) to grandmas or other unsuspecting clients. For example, regulators recently forced one large bank to shut down their private banking activities in Japan based on regulatory violations.

Career Potential

Many juniors in risk management aspire to work in the front office as a sales person, trader, etc. However, these transitions are generally rare and require much effort to pull off. Candidates must not only be outstanding, but they have to prove it as well. Perhaps more difficult still is maneuvering political hurdles. Managers naturally do not like to let go of good employees and their egos can also get in the way. Risk management provides a good bird's eye view of different businesses and how they are run, which is very valuable experience. However, leveraging it externally generally requires significant expertise in that area.

Key Factors

Risk management can be a slippery slope. Some positions can be challenging and require strong aptitude or strategic thought; but many risk management positions can be quite monotonous and reside in back office cubicles. The cushy hours and library-like atmosphere works for some but not all. The department is often viewed as the police of the firm (along with compliance perhaps). Enforcing risk limits or making inquiries with traders is no cake walk as traders can view these efforts as an impediment to making money. It is trading that runs the show in general so the police do not always have the final word.

Pros

- Money better than many non-finance jobs
- Very reasonable hours for finance
- Good exposure to business operations
- Relaxed atmosphere (back office)

Cons

- Back-office, non-revenue generating function
- Often cubicle environment
- Police function, not always respected by traders
- Career prospects effectively limited

Buy-side junior PM

Duties and Responsibilities

This is the buy-side equivalent of a trader. Junior PM positions are very similar to starting on a trading desk as one must learn trading systems, risk management, and all of the administrative details that trading involves.

Junior PMs are tucked under senior PMs who often tell them what to do. Naturally this is essentially anything that makes their lives easier. This could be executing transactions, confirming trades, researching ideas, reading news and research, performing some analyses, etc. The ultimate goal is to manage a portfolio of securities or positions and make a profit (unless it is a passive fund which tracks a benchmark).

One could perhaps break down a buy-side portfolio manager's job into four primary efforts: assessing individual investment opportunities, executing and unwinding trades, managing portfolio risk attributes, and all of the administrative work required to support the entire process. The simpler and more tedious tasks will be delegated to the junior PM and outsourced where possible (eg, to an execution or research team).

As this is not necessarily a quant or research position, technical skills are not always required but almost always helpful. Excel is probably sufficient for most tasks but there are some funds or portfolios that require more quantitative rigor.

As with sell-side trading, days generally start early so PMs can catch up on news and events relevant to their portfolio. They must also wrap up any work from the previous day such as reconciling trades or other figures.

Career Potential

Junior PMs generally want to be senior PMs, but they can also move over to the sell-side in proprietary trading or market making roles. Within their own organization they can also attempt to climb the corporate ladder into management. While this may allow for them to contribute more to strategic initiatives, the end goal is usually to become a partner or principal in the firm (ie, own a share of the profits).

Key Factors

As with trading, the main requirement for getting into portfolio management is being able to manage risk. It is important to remain objective and make rational investment decisions even when markets are selling off or rallying, not cracking under the pressure or becoming overconfident. It is also important to be able to assess which trades are good and which are bad. Brokers will no doubt shower you with ideas. Success follows the "do or die" mantra and poor performance is generally not tolerated for long. The hours can be long, but the rewards can more than compensate. Getting wined, dined, and entertained (eg, sporting events) by brokers can help make the experience more enjoyable too.

Pros
−   Money can be very good
−   Fast track career potential for quality candidates
−   Brokers kiss your ass and take you out

Cons
−   Hours can be long and include early starts
−   Many details to look after, both in the markets and administrative
−   Potential for high stress
−   "do or die"

Buy-side research

Duties and Responsibilities

Depending upon the size of the institution, buy-side research roles can amount to either a cog in a large machine or a real contributor working directly with a PM. For small firms, these roles can be very dynamic and involve a range of responsibilities. For larger firms with established research teams, it will feel more like a sell-side research position.

Just as with the sell-side, buy-side analysts can be macro, fundamental, or quantitative in focus, so specific duties will differ accordingly. Nonetheless, junior analysts will often be required to do due diligence, acquire data and information for analysis, and package into a format that they or someone else can use. Overall, the tasks and responsibilities will be very similar to that of a sell-side researcher but with two main distinctions.

While much of the sell-side research must be pretty and includes commentaries and marketing material, buy-side research is more narrowly focused on finding profitable trades. This can create increased pressure as buy-side research translates into trades that could lose money.

The other distinction being that much of the research can be directed towards portfolio analysis. This could be assessing correlations, volatilities, or other factors that contribute to the risk of the portfolio. It could also be backward looking in attributing profits and losses to those same or different factors.

Career Potential

Many buy-side research analysts want to eventually move into a Junior PM or PM role. Most buy-side firms will recognize quality employees and promote them in the direction they prefer. Larger firms may behave more like sell-side firms though, throwing more political hurdles in the way. Buy-side analysts can also move to other firms, perhaps over to the sell-side, though the normal flow of employees is from sell- to buy-side.

Key Factors

Buy-side research positions are similar to sell-side positions in that you must be able to work and think independently, but there is often an increased focus on results that might get lost in a larger sell-size research department. Doing what you are told and working with data may be prevalent in the early stages, but performance and out of the box thinking is critical for advancement. While there may be less regular supervision, hard work and solid contributions are more likely to pay-off and might require longer hours.

<u>Pros</u>
– Good pay potential for top performers
– Fast track opportunities
– Excellent exposure to the investment business

<u>Cons</u>
– Potential to be overwhelmed by multiple tasks
– Increased pressure and stress since work translates into profits or losses

Other

Overview

In this section we are referring to businesses such as retail or commercial banking and some parts of the brokerage business. These are businesses that generally focus on just a few core products or services and then leverage them amongst as many customers as possible. They invest in systems which give them an economy of scale for processing and managing their transactions. The core business revolves around managing processes, increasing efficiency where possible, and increasing volume. Indeed, for these businesses the key to profits is generally through volume, not speculation, managing risk, or mega-deals.

In general, these businesses tend to be less dynamic than the others we have just highlighted. Even dynamic individuals with loads of aptitude are going to be unlikely to change the core machinery except in some rare instances. Accordingly, upward mobility is often motivated more by the number of years worked than merit. We find these businesses, on average, have less upside potential in terms of promotion and compensation.

This is a gross generalization of course. We are not saying that exciting or well paid careers do not exist in these types of businesses. Indeed, there are usually some pockets of opportunity within. We simply feel that opportunities are rare and the atmosphere often provides more headwind for advancing careers.

Career Potential

Picking the right role is all the more important. The sales roles within these businesses, for example, will generally be well paid, but not exorbitantly so. There are also a few trading desks since loan portfolios must be managed and there are various research units working on credit scoring, portfolio analytics, etc. The key point is that roles within these businesses will earn significantly less on average and will be less dynamic than the other roles we've described. It is worth noting that retail and commercial banks recycle (sell) many of their risks (eg, loans, credit card debts, mortgages, etc) to banks whose dedicated structuring/trading desks repackage them (see Appendix C: The Collateralized Debt Obligation (CDO)), so there is some valuable experience to be had.

Key Factors

Candidates considering jobs within these areas should avoid commoditized roles and exercise extra caution to ensure that their positions have potential for career advancement and good compensation. Prepare for a long, slow grind otherwise. Despite this, while these types of jobs do not have the same upside or fast track potential as the others we described, most jobs in the financial industry pay more than similar roles outside. So pay is still good by most standards.

Pros
– Less stress on average
– Potential ego boost if you're sharper than most of your colleagues

Cons
– Seniority often trumps merit
– Pay not exceptional
– Less dynamic roles
– Cubicle work environment likely

4.2 Job Compatibility Scoring System

This section is meant to be used as a tool to help assess how compatible one is for different roles. We have created ten categories, each of which describes either required skill sets or characteristics of the roles. For clarity, **higher or lower scores are not necessarily better** but are used to indicate the strength of attribute. We score each role on a scale of 1-5 in each category. The categories are as follows:

Figure 15: Job Compatibility Attributes and Descriptions

Attribute	Description
Quantitative ability	Basic numeracy is assumed. This describes the grasp of concepts such as basic statistics & time series, calculus, linear algebra, and perhaps stochastic calculus.
Analytical thinking / logical reasoning	Ability to assess situations or analyses by decomposing them into critical their elements and then using logical reasoning to generate potential action points or solutions
Computing	Basic computing skills assumed (eg, email and word processing). This describes further understanding of spreadsheets, programming, databases, and other computing tools.
Communication skills	Ability to listen and absorb, convey thoughts in a concise and coherent manner, candidly discuss difficult topics, and present to groups or large audiences.
Social skills	Ability to readily interact with colleagues and clients of all sorts that you do or do not know, strike up or maintain conversations, and make new acquaintances in person or on the phone.
Writing skills	Basic writing skills assumed. Ability to write messages (eg, email) in a quick and concise manner, or produce structured documents and presentations that efficiently convey a specific message.
Learning curve	One's learning curve is often a trait defined by each individual. Some roles are more isolated or repetitive than others and not conducive to continual learning. Other roles are more dynamic, change focus and promote learning.
Work load / hours	Standard full time hours (eg, 40 hours/week) are likely the minimum. Lower scores indicate workloads closer to this minimum. Higher scores indicate late nights and weekends.
Stress level	Lower scores indicate a quieter, more relaxed work environment. Higher scores indicate more constant decision making, deadline pressures and/or a more hectic work environment.
Compensation	Minimum compensation levels are assumed to be competitive with those outside the financial services. This scale is relative to other jobs in the financial services industry.

Note: These categories and scores were constructed to describe the junior roles described in this chapter. They apply to the zero to three year experience range. It is worth noting that we did not include an economics or financial background category. This might seem ironic given this book is about careers in financial services. There are two reasons for this.

The first reason is that this book targets people who do not necessarily have these backgrounds. Hence, the first half of this book is devoted to the financial markets and related financial institutions. The second and perhaps more important reason we did not include these categories is that few, if any, groups specifically require economics backgrounds outside of economics research. The same could also be argued for finance degrees and corporate finance. Employers are primarily interested in aptitude, communications skills, and ability to complete projects (we discuss this in the next chapter). Banks, for example, generally have their own training programs to impart much of the required financial knowledge unto their junior employees.

Figure 16: Job Compatibility Scores

Role	Sub -Role	Quant ability	Anal/log reason	Comp-uting	Comm skills	Social skills	Writing skills	Learning curve	Workload/ hours	Stress	Comp/ pay
Corp finance		3	4	3	5	4	3	5	5	5	5
Capital mkts		3	4	3	4	3	4	5	5	5	5
Sales	Cash	2	2	3	5	5	3	3	4	4	5
	Flow deriv	3	3	3	5	5	3	3	4	4	5
	Struc deriv	3	4	3	5	5	4	4	4	3	5
Trading	Cash	3	4	4	2	2	2	3	3	5	5
	Flow deriv	4	4	4	3	2	2	4	4	5	5
	Exotic	4	5	4	3	2	2	4	4	5	5
	Prop	4	5	4	2	2	2	5	4	5	5
Research	Macro	3	4	4	4	3	5	5	4	3	4
	Fundmtl	3	4	4	4	3	5	5	4	3	4
	Quant	4	4	5	4	3	5	5	4	3	4
Structuring		4	4	4	3	4	4	4	5	4	5
Risk mgt	Monitoring	4	3	3	4	3	3	3	4	3	3
	Research	4	4	4	4	3	4	3	4	2	3
Analytics		5	5	5	3	2	3	4	2	2	4
Buy-side	Junior PM	4	4	4	4	3	2	5	5	5	5
	Research	4	4	4	3	4	4	5	4	3	4

Chapter 4 Concepts

- Broad idea of various roles
- 'Volume' focused businesses
- Required skill sets (quantitative, analytical, computing, communication, etc)
- Career potential
- Learning curve
- Workload and required hours
- Stress levels (deadlines, berating, etc)
- Compensation

Chapter 5:

Quantitative Roles

While this chapter primarily targets those with quantitative backgrounds, it may also be useful to others. Understanding the roles and functions of other groups is often important since you will likely need to leverage their expertise and resources at some point. Becoming familiar or brushing up on quantitative concepts will make you a more well rounded candidate.

5.1 Roadmap

Before we delve into the roles and tasks that quants are generally involved in, we include two brief background sections. The first lays out our definition of a quant to avoid any potential confusion with other definitions. The second section explains some of the limitations to modeling that quants (and those using the models!) should be aware of. Financial markets do not necessarily conform to models or formulas so it is extremely dangerous not to be aware of these limitations.

After these two sections, the core focus of this chapter is on the roles and activities that require a quantitative background. We first highlight a number of relevant mathematical and financial concepts ranging from simple bond math to derivatives pricing. Then we use this as a foundation to discuss the specific areas where quantitative skills are needed for each role, making concrete links between the financial applications and the required mathematics.

5.1.1 What is a Quant?

The terms quant and PhD (in a technical discipline) are often used synonymously. Here we use broader definition of the term *quant*. We are not confining ourselves to PhD or advanced degrees, but referring to anyone with at least a BS level degree in a technical area, be it in mathematics, physics, engineering, statistics, etc.

In the following, we focus on roles for which managers specifically seek quantitative backgrounds. This roughly translates into a score of either 4 or 5 in the "quantitative ability" category from Chapter 4. While there is no universal hierarchy of quantitative skills, we could intuitively define our "quantitative ability" scale as follows:

1 – Skills associated with the "I hate math" crowd
2 – Capable of accounting math (+ - * /), but not necessarily comfortable with much more
3 – More than numerate, quick with figures and perhaps comfortable with basic statistics
4 – Solid math background. Newtonian calculus, differential equations, perhaps some linear algebra
5 – Advanced technical degree. Comfortable with stochastic calculus and/ or numerical methods

5.1.2 Theory Versus Practice

One of the biggest issues that math and related majors must accept is that the models they develop and work with in finance are only approximations. Some models are more reliable than others, but even the most frequently used models can breakdown. This frequently occurs when financial markets are under duress. So there is no guaranteed formula for the price of any asset, whether it is a cash asset (eg, stocks and bonds) or a derivative, as this would imply deterministic and hence predictable performance. There are two primary reasons for this in my view.

The first reason is that most models make assumptions that simply do not hold all of the time. This is the case with derivatives pricing models. For example, some models assume fixed interest rates, volatility, dividends, etc. when these quantities actually are not static. While many of these issues are addressed by new models, few account for transactions costs which are almost always left to the discretion of the trader to figure out.

The second reason that models and formulas cannot always work is that there is a psychological element to pricing. During stable or bull markets, investors attach liquidity premiums to different securities. That is, they will pay less for those which they cannot easily liquidate. During market sell offs, people tend to be more risk averse and unwilling to pay as much for stocks because they believe they are too risky.

Models should be robust enough that they provide value (eg, profits) when markets are stable or rallying and do not lose too much when markets are unstable. At very least, any market participant who is using models for investing or trading purposes should be aware that the model is only approximate and has limitations. History has exposed many models (traders, businesses, and companies too!) as being inadequate in this respect; they often make money consistently when markets are stable or rising, but then they lose all of those profits and sometimes more when markets turn for the worse. Consider a casino that offers a game where the players roll a normal six-sided die and get paid whatever number they roll except for six, in which case they have to pay the casino 16. The players will win most (5/6 = 83.3%) of the time, but will money lose on average (expected payout = $\frac{1}{6} \times 1 + \frac{1}{6} \times 2 + \frac{1}{6} \times 3 + \frac{1}{6} \times 4 + \frac{1}{6} \times 5 + \frac{1}{6} \times (-16) = -\frac{1}{6}$).

5.2 Quantitative Concepts and the Roles That Require Them

Now our goal is to familiarize the reader with roles that require quantitative backgrounds. In particular, we explain specific financial applications within each role that require varying degrees of mathematical skills. We do this by explaining a variety of financial and mathematical concepts in this first section. That is, we highlight the mathematics – ranging from simple to complex – behind some of the most common (and a few uncommon) financial applications. We then go through each of the roles to which we assigned a quantitative ability score of 4 or 5. For each role, we explain which quantitative (and financial) concepts apply and are most often required.

5.2.1 Essential Concepts

Our focus here is on the mathematical skills that are required for various roles. We could just make a list of different mathematical concepts, but this would do nothing to further most people's knowledge since most of these generic skills are highlighted in text books, jobs listings, and other resources. Our approach is slightly different. In particular, we expect that the quantitative reader has purchased this book so that they can get a better understanding of the financial contexts for their skill sets. Accordingly, we proceed by first highlighting and explaining the financial concepts, and then describing some of the associated mathematics. While there is no universal classification to follow, we break up the financial applications into three categories: Asset pricing, portfolio analysis, and derivatives.

<u>Asset pricing:</u> Asset pricing is actually a very broad topic so we will confine our discussion to the core topic of cash flow analysis. In particular, we will show how this basic valuation tool is used in the pricing of government bonds (which are typically assumed to be risk free since governments ultimately can print their own money), corporate bonds, and equities.

The *time value of money* is the underlying principle here; a dollar is worth more if you have it today than if you receive it a week, month, year, etc later. If you have it today then you have the ability to use it if/when you come across an opportunity you find attractive. But if you do not have it until some later date, you will forego potential opportunities. As a result, if you place your money with a relatively safe[34] institution such as a bank or the government, they will be obliged to pay you some extra money, called *interest*, to compensate you for this time value. The level of interest is quoted as an annual percentage of the total amount of money and is called an *interest rate*. The interest rate you receive depends on how long you agree to lend your money to them.

The mathematics around interest and time value of money are simple. While we do not spell out precise formulas, we use examples to illustrate most concepts. The first example here demonstrates what is called a *simple interest* calculation. If you lend $100 at an interest rate of 5% for six months, then they should pay you back $100 \times [\, 1 + 5\% \times 0.5 \,] = \$102.50$. Since the money was not lent out for the entire year, one does not receive the entire 5% of interest. The 0.5 in this calculation represents the six months as 0.5 years. It is worth noting that there are different *day count conventions* to account for time (eg, total number of days versus number of business days) that we are brushing under the rug to keep things simple. This can also be viewed from another angle. If we were to receive $100 in 18 months time and the associated interest rate was still 5%, this should be worth $\$100 \div [\, 1 + 5\% \times 1.5 \,] = \$93.02$ to us today. This $100 is said to be *discounted* to its *present value*.

---

34   We assume for the sake of explanation that these entities will pay you back in full though it is not entirely guaranteed.

Valuing cash flows can also be done by *compounding* interest. In this case, interest is calculated at intermediate points, added to the total notional, and then future interest is calculated based on this new higher notional. For example, if a bond (or borrower) indicates that it pays 5% semi-annually, an 18 month investment of $100 would end up being worth $100 × $[1 + 5\% \div 2]^3$ = $107.69 at the end of the 18 months. The interest is applied every six months (ie, three times over 18 months) at a rate of 2.5% (5% ÷ 2 to de-annualize the 5% figure). There are many resources that explain these calculations in greater detail but we highly recommend Frank Fabozzi's book entitled "Fixed Income Mathematics" which covers this and much more.

Quick comment: Some people with derivatives experience may notice that we do not use the exponential function for the compounding or discounting calculations. Real financial calculations do not. The reason the exponential function is commonly used in derivatives pricing and related calculations is because it makes the derivations and formulas much simpler. The exponential function has favorable properties when it comes to mathematical derivatives and integrations. Using simple interest calculations would make most formulas explode and probably make closed form solutions impossible for many derivative contracts.

Armed with this *discounted cash flow* (DCF) approach, one can easily calculate the value of many bonds. Take for example a bond that pays $6 interest annually every year for five years after which it repays the principal (ie, the original amount or notional, in this case $100). There are six cash flows at five different times: five bond coupons of $6 and the final $100 repayment. Assuming interest rates are 5%, the present value of this bond is $6 ÷ $[1 + 5\%]^1$ + $6 ÷ $[1 + 5\%]^2$ + $6 ÷ $[1 + 5\%]^3$ + $6 ÷ $[1 + 5\%]^4$ + $6 ÷ $[1 + 5\%]^5$ + $100 ÷ $[1 + 5\%]^5$ = $104.33.

Quick comment: There is one very clear relationship that emerges from bond pricing that should be well understood: *the price of a bond and its yield are inversely related.* As the price goes up, the yield goes down. As the price goes down, the yield goes up.

Figure 17: Discounted Cash Flow Illustration

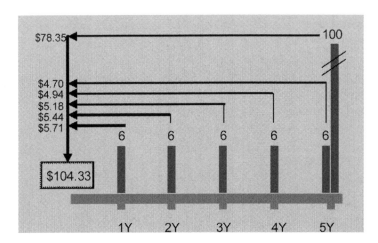

Next we extend our approach to bonds issued by corporations which are more risky. Because they entail risks that the bonds above did not (recall that corporations can default or go bankrupt), they must compensate investors accordingly. If two bonds are the same price but one is more risky than the other, the riskier bond will pay higher coupons. If two bonds offer to pay the same coupons, the riskier bond will be cheaper[35].

To keep things simple, let's consider a one year $100 bond with no coupons. Furthermore, let's make a few assumptions:

- the (risk free) interest rate is still 5%
- the probability of the company defaulting (ie, not paying all of the money back) is 10%
- if the company defaults, it will sell off all of its assets and pay back half of the loan (that is, the assumed *recovery rate* is 50%)

Given the uncertainty of the situation, we use an expected value to assess the value of the bond. Otherwise, the discounted cash flow calculations are precisely the same as before. In the scenario where the company does not default, we will get paid $100 in one year's time. The present value of this is $100 ÷ [1 + 5%]¹ = $95.24. In the case where the company defaults, we will receive $50 in one year's time and this is works out to $47.62. Given there is a 90%

---

35   This assumes the same maturity and timing of cash flows.

chance of the former and 10% of the latter situation, our expected value is $0.9 \times \$95.24 + 0.1 \times \$47.62 = \$90.48$.

Another way to look at this is to back out the discount in terms of an increased interest rate. In other words, what interest rate would it take to discount $100 to $90.48 (ignoring the potential default scenario for now)? This works out to 10.52%. Accordingly, the additional 5.52% of interest accounts for the potential default scenario. This quantity is called a *credit spread*. We can value risky bonds if we are given the credit spread or the default probability (note that we are assuming a recovery rate of 50%). Default probabilities are not easy to calculate but there are many models and tools that attempt to do so. We also made the assumption that investors would still receive half of their money back in the case of a default, and this *recovery rate* is also far from certain.

In the bond market, only the terms of the contracts (ie, the timing and amounts of cash flows) and their prices are observable. The default probability or recovery rate can only be implied (ie, backed out) if the other is known or assumed. Company fundamentals such as leverage, assets, profitability, etc are commonly used to estimate one or both of these figures. Plugging such estimates into the cash flow formulas above generates a price which can then be compared with the market price to judge whether it is cheap or expensive (relative to the model price). However, we must note that this approach is quite simplified. For example, we completely neglected the timing of a default and corresponding payments as they are also uncertain. There are many other models and nobody is to say which one is the best at any given time.

Inconsistencies between model prices and market prices are often attributed to another factor called the *risk premium*. This quantity is widely heard but incredibly ambiguous. It broadly refers to the additional discounting of cash flows which compensate investors specifically for taking risk. Note that if risky and non-risky bonds are priced as above, their expected returns are the same (and equal to the interest rate). Cynically speaking, the risk premium is essentially a convenient quantity used to make the models more accurate. In the end, we can fit any data given enough variables!

The last application of this cash flow analysis we discuss is in the context of equities (stocks). We can look at any company, business, project, etc simply as a stream of cash flows and value it accordingly. However, unlike the pre-specified payments for bonds, these cash flows are always uncertain (not just due to defaults). As a result, more assumptions are required.

Some of these assumptions revolve around growth. In particular, the cash flows under consideration are assumed to grow at a specific rate for a specific period of time. Another assumption is required to stipulate the discount rate to be applied to the cash flows. Given the historical out-performance of equities over bonds (though the credit crisis may alter this conclusion), many people assign an *equity risk premium* (precisely same notion as above) to further discount cash flows.

Another question arises out of what cash flows should be analyzed for a company. Some forecast and use a stream of earnings (accounting profits) as cash flows. Others, distrustful of accounting methods, might use the cash that is actually generated by the business. Still, others use the dividend stream since it is the real cash investors would receive. In any case, the point is that the choice of cash flows to analyze makes a huge difference.

Readers interested in delving further into this discounted cash flow approach for equities should investigate the *Gordon growth model* as we do not provide example calculations here. All of these assumptions effectively make this approach more art than science and the same can probably be said of other approaches to analyzing equities such as ratios and peer comparisons (eg, comparing P/E and other ratios).

All of the mathematics required for the analyses above are very basic. However, there is another field in which many investors build more complex models and use them to construct equity portfolios or to highlight potential opportunities when they arise. This area of investing is called *quantitative equity*. Similar approaches are probably used for other asset classes (eg, credit) but we believe the quantitative effort within equities is the most popular.

Aside from using models to screen for individual opportunities, one could divide quantitative equity research into two primary applications: long only and relative value portfolios. Given the uncertainty surrounding the prediction of absolute share prices, many of these models are geared towards estimating relative, rather than absolute, value. It is worth noting that many hedge funds and bank proprietary trading desks run significantly sized long-short portfolios based on quant equity models.

A standard approach for quantitative equity modeling might be to regress fundamental factors (eg, balance sheets and income statement figures, ratios thereof, etc) against share prices at different points in time[36]. Once the fitted model is calculated, it could be applied to current fundamental data to assess which stocks are cheap or expensive relative to their fundamentals[37]. A more complex approach might be to feed a neural network similar data and effectively create a "black box" model to ranking stocks or predicting their direction.

Some models also integrate technical analysis. That is, instead of using fundamental information and comparing it to the share price, one would analyze only the price and volume (amount traded) to estimate future directions. This approach is generally labeled *technical analysis*. It involves notions such as momentum, support and resistance levels, and a variety of different patterns that assets presumably follow.

My explanations above are really gross simplifications. But the point is that there is a broad field of investment strategies utilizing mathematics ranging from simple regressions to complex neural networks. While we just described an example involving equities, similar types of models are applied across asset classes. Additionally, much of the analysis in this field is devoted to looking at portfolios as a whole, not just as individual assets, and this leads us to the next topic.

Portfolio analysis: Because there is such a broad spectrum of topics that could fall under the heading *portfolio analysis*, we first summarize what this area encompasses and then discuss two popular areas of portfolio analysis that utilize some elegant mathematics: *efficient frontiers* and *transition matrices*.

Generally speaking, portfolio analysis addresses issues regarding risk for portfolios of assets (stocks, bonds, businesses, properties, etc). Of central importance to almost all portfolio analyses is *correlation*. Even if you have a good grasp of each individual security, correlation will dictate how the assets will move in conjunction with each other and how the portfolio as a whole is affected. And that is usually the goal, to assess risk at the portfolio level. Here are some questions correlation helps address:

---

36   Such strategies are sometimes called *quantamental* since they utilize quantitative models and fundamental data.
37   This is just a simple example; ordinary least squares regressions are often misapplied and abused.

- How volatile will the overall portfolio be?
- What weightings will produce the optimal risk/return trade-off
- What is the maximum drawdown?
- How liquid is the portfolio?
- What risk does it have to particular factors such as sectors or regions, inflation, interest rates, credit spreads, GDP, etc.
- What cash flows (eg, dividends, bond coupons, etc) will it generate?

This list names just a few of the reasons portfolio analysis is required. It is important to realize that this does not only refer to the needs of investment managers, but also CEOs and other executives analyzing portfolios of business units.

The first portfolio analysis tool we describe is the *efficient frontier*. This is basically a two-dimensional plot of risk and return for various combinations of assets. Naturally, an investor, portfolio manager, or CEO will want the best return for a given level of risk (volatility). The mathematics behind this are actually quite elegant, but the analysis inevitably requires forward looking inputs which are difficult to estimate. In particular, there are three crucial ingredients: expected returns, volatilities, and correlations. Mathematically speaking, this would be a vector of returns, a vector of volatilities, and a matrix of correlations.

Figure 18: Generic Efficient Frontier Illustration

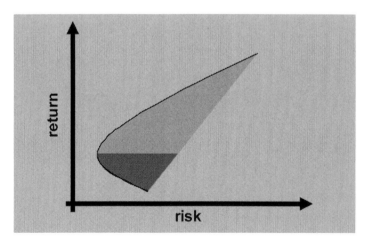

Regardless of the portfolio type or its purpose, estimating asset prices (which is more or less equivalent to the expected returns) of financial assets is a fuzzy science as we just discussed in the previous section. While some practitioners employ their models or analysts to provide this information, others invoke the *efficient markets hypothesis*[38] which nullifies any efforts to estimate returns or value assets. Forecasting volatility is not straightforward either. Most people use historical volatility levels or those implied from the derivatives markets. In either case, this parameter can change quickly.

Just like returns and volatilities, it is not easy to forecast the co-relationships between assets, though some might argue that estimating the correlations between *factors* is more reliable. In this case, one would express a portfolio of assets as a portfolio of weighted factors. Mathematically, this amounts to a *change of basis*. But not matter how you do it, this simply inserts one more floor into this house of cards.

Quick comment: I am clearly not a fan of these models and believe that the "garbage in, garbage out" rule applies. Despite my opinion, many people wholeheartedly believe in these types of models and they are widely used throughout the industry.

Once the above quantities are provided, a mean-variance optimization (MVO) is used to create the efficient frontier. That is, it will identify the weighting combinations that can be used to create the portfolios with the best risk and reward. For a single period application as just described, quadratic programming can be used to generate the solution (ie, the efficient frontier). However, for multi-period applications, non-linear solutions are often needed, though there are some further assumptions that still allow a quadratic solution.

The example we just described is just one core approach. We could change constraints – perhaps allow for short positions (negative weights) or caps on weightings – or change the objective function being optimized (eg, entropic measures). Naturally these lead to more challenging solutions that must be balanced with practicality.

---

38   The *efficient markets hypothesis* effectively assumes that all information is instantly priced into the markets. As a corollary, no investor would be able to accurately forecast returns.

Another mathematically elegant portfolio analysis tool is *transition matrices*. The original and primary application is for measuring risk in credit portfolios (portfolios of corporate loans, bonds, etc). This effort was pioneered by risk management professionals at JPMorgan in the 1990s and subsequently spun off into its own company called RiskMetrics. Given that they document most all of this framework in their technical documents which are available for free on the web, we provide a brief overview but do not go into deep detail on any of the calculations.

This framework first requires that bonds first be classified according to a rating system with associated default probabilities; a higher rating yields a lower default probability. Let's assume there are N such ratings[39]. Then a transition matrix can be constructed as an N x N+1 matrix whose entries $P[i,j]$ define the probability of a bond with a rating i becoming a bond of rating j. Note the +1 in N+1 allows for an additional column where a rated bond can transition into a default (but defaulted bonds cannot transition out of default).

Assuming that the transition probabilities are static (or specifying another transition matrix for a different period) allows one to simply multiply the matrices to generate a multi-period transition matrix. As a result, one can estimate bond values and volatilities with the probability distributions that the matrix yields[40]. While the expected values can be summed to get an expected value of a portfolio, estimating portfolio volatility requires some sort of joint probabilities between the assets.

Correlation arises here again. One approach that some people have used is to assume that the companies' underlying asset returns are normally distributed. Then one can specify a correlation matrix and use it to calculate the resultant distribution for the portfolio. One of the primary applications of this framework is to generate loss distributions and ultimately compute Value at Risk (V@R). Note that a loss (or profit) distribution is just a translated distribution of future portfolio values since it is simply the future minus original value.

Given the large size of loan portfolios, this task is naturally a computational challenge. Such calculations rely on some assumptions that did not necessar-

---

39   These are denoted with cryptic labels that look like AAA, Baa, Ba1, etc depending upon the rating agency and risk of the bond.

40   Note that we brushed the impact of recovery rates for defaulted bonds as well as interim cash flows paid by the bonds under the rug.

ily conform to or reconcile with market prices, thus making their accuracy questionable. However, in the context of providing daily risk (V@R) figures to management, this probably can be tolerated, especially since the calculations can be run overnight and management knows that the figures are only estimates.

As most people are now aware, the credit market experienced massive growth over the last decade. In particular, collateralized debt obligations (CDOs) and related credit derivative products have exploded (well, in terms of growth but just realized my unintended pun). We provide a brief overview of these products in *Appendix C: The Collateralized Debt Obligation (CDO)*. Traders and market participants needed more accurate and timely calculations since they were actually buying and selling products that required estimates of joint distributions (correlations). As a result, extraordinary efforts have gone into developing new models for pricing and hedging these products. Base correlations and copula models are some examples, but there has been a huge surge of research in this field. The interested reader can easily find numerous academic papers on the web.

Derivatives: Derivatives is probably the area that is most widely known for hiring quants. Indeed, the core models used in the context of pricing, hedging, and analyzing derivatives generally require stronger quantitative backgrounds.

The first concept that we explain is the *no-arbitrage principle*. Arbitrage refers to the ability to make riskless profits[41] and the no-arbitrage principle stipulates that prices should not allow arbitrage situations to exist (as people would jump on them and they would disappear, usually very quickly).

For example, consider a 3-month future[42] on an asset that yields no interest or dividends. Let's suppose this asset costs $100 today and interest rates are 4%. The price of the future, which entitles ownership to the asset three months later, will not reflect expectations of where the asset price will be in three months. Instead, its price will be determined in such a way that nobody can ar-

---

41   In practice, there really are no truly riskless profits. Transactions will be required and they will always involve execution or settlement risk. That said, we will use the term *arbitrage* to describe opportunities to make money without market or credit risk.

42   For those who are not familiar with this derivative contract please see *Appendix B: Four Very Common Derivatives*.

bitrage the future against the asset. In this case, the future will be priced at $101; any other price will lead to an arbitrage situation. If the future trades at a price of $102, someone can borrow $100 and purchase the asset today, then deliver it in three months time for $102, pay back their loan $100 + $1 of interest (4% for three months), and have a dollar leftover as profit. Conversely, someone could execute the reverse transaction if the future traded below $101.

Traders who buy and sell futures to usually do not just sit on their hands after the transaction and hope the market goes in their direction. They will quickly, if not simultaneously, set up the offsetting transactions. Of particular importance here is that once a trader sells a future and hedges himself (borrows and buys the asset), he does not care which way the asset moves. It does not matter because he knows that he will be selling it later at a pre-specified price.

The point of this example is simply that the prices of derivative securities are determined by this no-arbitrage principle. In other words, the price of a derivative will be equal to the cost of replicating or hedging it. Once you have setup the corresponding transactions that will replicate what you have bought or sold, you have neutralized yourself to the risk of the asset moving up or down in price. This approach is often called the *risk neutral* pricing framework.

For futures, the mathematics is mostly very simple. There are some exceptions though. Bond futures are one example. Many bond futures stipulate types of underlying bonds as opposed to a specific bond to be delivered at the expiration of the future. Accordingly, the seller of such a futures contract will generally find the bond that meets the specifications but is *cheapest to deliver*. As a result, there is some uncertainty involved which translates into *optionality* for the seller of the future. We do not delve into this here as it can easily be found on the web.

This leads us into the next and perhaps most significant development in derivatives pricing: the Black-Scholes framework for pricing options. This is probably the most extensively covered topic in financial mathematics, almost certainly so if one includes subsequent extensions of this seminal work.

The core development of this framework was that options and other derivatives could still be priced using the risk neutral approach. It simply required a few further assumptions regarding movements of the asset and dynamic hedging (note that the future replication was static). In particular, they assumed the underlying asset followed a geometric Brownian motion and that hedging could be performed continuously and without transaction costs. This hedging is called *delta hedging* and we discuss it momentarily. It is also worth noting that any directional expectations of the underlying asset (embodied in a *drift term* for the Brownian process) do not impact the derivative price, just as with the case of pricing the future contract above. Indeed, the dynamic hedging removes directional risk at every instant and any expectation (drift term) elegantly falls out of the calculations.

While these assumptions do not perfectly match reality, the model was a vast improvement over previous attempts to price options and is still the core model used within most of today's pricing models. There have been many such extensions that have attempted to improve this core model which include the integration of jump processes, stochastic volatility and interest rates (fixed volatility and interest rates were originally assumed), etc.

Most of the inputs into vanilla derivative pricing models are fairly straightforward (eg, stock price and interest rates) except volatility – though dividends have become a focal point as well. Most pricing models still do not account for skew or term structure of volatility. As a result, traders maintain *volatility surfaces* which prescribe different volatility inputs for different strikes and maturities.

As we mentioned above, this framework assumed that the hedge could be dynamically maintained. The purpose of this hedge was to offset a derivative's exposure to the underlying. The derivative naturally derives its payout and hence its value from the price of the underlying security. The size (and sign) of this hedge (ie, the hedge ratio) corresponds to how much the derivative price moves when the underlying itself moves. This is precisely the first derivative (of the option price with respect to the underlying) and is called *delta*. Consequently, this process is called *delta hedging*.

As we noted above, the Black-Scholes model, nor any of its extensions, is perfect. Residual risks remain and must be managed accordingly. In other words, delta is just of many risk factors traders monitor and manage. The other sensitivities are calculated in precisely the same way (using mathematical derivatives) and are broadly called the *greeks*. Aside from delta, rho, mu, vega, and gamma are the most popular. We briefly summarize these below:

- **Delta:** 1st derivative of the option price with respect to the underlying. This is generally the primary risk to be hedged.
- **Gamma:** 2nd derivative of the option price with respect to the underlying. The textbook definition is not practical. Gamma really indicates the exposure to *realized volatility*[43].
- **Vega:** 1st derivative of the option price with respect to the volatility (usually called *implied volatility*). Many professional investors specifically isolate this exposure in order to speculate on volatility as an asset.
- **Theta:** 1st derivative of the option price with respect to time. That is, it indicates the amount of change in the option price per one day lapsing (ie, shorter maturity).
- **Rho:** 1st derivative of the option price with respect to the interest rate.
- **Mu:** 1st derivative of the option price with respect to the dividends.

Black-Scholes is really just a starting point for derivatives pricing and risk management modeling. Most firms that deal in derivatives will develop their own derivatives pricing models and work to continually improve them. This area probably boasts the most well known type of quant job known to mankind. Working in this area requires a sophisticated quantitative background. Modeling derivatives involves a variety of mathematical tools including stochastic process, differential equations and numerical methods. As this topic is already extensively covered in books, papers, classrooms, and on the web, we do not discuss it further here. We do, however, suggest either (or both) Nassim Taleb's *Dynamic Hedging* or Salih Neftci's *Principles of Financial Engineering* for core modeling approaches. For more recent developments, readers should consult www.wilmott.com as it has many useful resources and forums devoted to these topics.

The area we just described could broadly be labeled risk neutral modeling and is 99.9% internally focused; the models are used to price and hedge derivatives products bought and sold by dealers. However, recall that this approach values derivatives based on how much it costs to hedge them and has nothing to do with forecasts or expectations. There is another entire spectrum of quantitative models that are devoted to derivatives for the purpose of speculation and profiting – as opposed to hedging.

---

43   We explain this further in *Appendix B: Four Very Common Derivatives.*

First, there are *delta-one*[44] derivatives which basically replicate the underlying cash asset. Just like our example above where we priced the future, there are many professional investors focused on arbitraging the difference between delta-one derivatives and the underling assets. This difference is often referred to as the *basis*. Mathematically, this is a tedious rather than complex business where computers are setup to do most of the work.

Derivatives with non-linear payoffs require a volatility input for their pricing (think of options as an intuitive example). And as we highlighted in our description of vega, many market practitioners on both the sell- and buy-side use such derivatives to speculate on *implied volatility* (ie, the volatility forecast input into the model to price options and other derivatives). Even though it is not a tangible asset that you can hold in your hands (like a bond or stock certificate), people speculate on it through the purchase and sale of derivatives which have volatility exposures[45]. Entire businesses have been built around trading volatility. This area is generally called *volatility arbitrage*[46] and is the focal point of much quantitative modeling.

In order to cater specifically to volatility trading professionals, banks and exchanges have developed specific products that focus solely on volatility. Two of the most popular such products are variance swaps and VIX futures, though there are many different variations and related products. We briefly describe variance swaps below but refer the reader to the Chicago Board Options Exchange website for more information on the VIX futures and related products.

In my view, variance swaps are one of the finest examples of financial engineering, both for the users of such instruments as well as the traders who hedge them. On the surface, they are relatively straightforward products which allow

---

44   Derivatives with payouts that are linear in the underlying are said to be *delta-one* instruments. The reason is that the delta of these instruments (unless they are leveraged) is basically one. This includes futures, forwards, equity swaps, ETFs (even though an ETF is technically not a derivative), etc.

45   We provide an introduction to volatility trading via options in *Appendix B: Four Very Common Derivatives* where we discuss some of the basic strategies to profit from volatility arbitrage.

46   While volatility arbitrage has gained much more popularity in recent years (probably because of the new products created to trade it), it is worth noting that volatility trading has roots in convertible bond arbitrage going back almost two decades.

investors to explicitly trade volatility (well, volatility *squared*). The final payout is simply $(\sigma^2 - \sigma_k^2) \cdot N$ where σ^2 is the realized variance over a period, σ_k^2 is the prιχe paid (variance strike), and N is the notional traded. Of particular importance, the investor who uses a variance swap (not the trader who hedges it) avoids most all of the hassle of dynamic hedging that would be required to trade volatility via options.

But it is behind the scenes in the risk neutral modeling where the real mathematical beauty lies. While simply expressed, the payout is actually exceedingly complex[47]. Accordingly, one cannot avoid appreciating how clean the hedging mechanics are. To replicate this payoff, the trader only needs to purchase one static portfolio of options and delta hedge them through maturity. This is the primary reason variance swaps evolved as the more liquid product; the hedge is much easier to implement. In order to replicate a volatility swap (just remove the squares in the above payout), the option portfolio is dynamic. That is, it requires frequent buying and selling of options which involves more issues such as transaction costs. While we do not delve into those calculations here, we suggest interested readers check out a seminal paper by Emmanuel Derman (http://www.ederman.com/new/docs/gs-volatility_swaps.pdf) for more information on variance swap products.

There are several other interesting directions to which volatility arbitrage can lead. One such route is correlation trading. Correlation trading has been very popular in recent years and many investors have made huge profits and losses speculating on correlation. While there are actually *correlation swap* products that make correlation trading straightforward, the most popular means to trade equity correlation[48] has been through *dispersion* trades. A typical dispersion trade will short correlation via long volatility positions in the constituents of an index and a short volatility position in the index itself. If correlations are low or negative, the stocks can move significantly, but the

---

47   It is easy to take this for granted. As simple as the volatility calculation may appear, it still depends on an average of the squared (log) returns of the underlying asset for each observation period (usually daily observations) over the period of the swap. This is vastly more complex that vanilla options payoffs which only depend on a terminal stock value and are piecewise linear.
48   Here we describe correlation trading for equities via equity derivatives, but correlation is also actively traded in other asset classes. As we discussed above, CDO valuations depend heavily on correlations and investors use those products to speculate on credit correlations as well.

index might not move so much (low/negative correlation ➔ more movements canceling each other out ➔ index does not move as much). As a result, the long stock volatility positions will benefit from higher stock volatility, but the short index volatility position would not suffer as volatility is muted at the index level.

Summary: The above three sections (asset pricing, portfolio analysis, and derivatives) are by no means an exhaustive treatment of financial or mathematical concepts found in the financial services industry. However, this treatment touches on the most popular topics and this should at very least serve as a good eye opener for the types of financial applications one will encounter and the related mathematics. In no particular order, these mathematics include but are not limited to:

- **Basic statistics:** Common distributions, correlation, and expectations
- **Newtonian calculus:** Mathematical derivatives and integrals
- **Differential equations:** Heat equation, Fourier transforms, Black-Scholes PDE
- **Linear algebra:** Systems of equations, invertibility, Eigen-values/vectors
- **Optimization:** Quadratic / non-linear / integer programming
- **Stochastic calculus:** Ito's lemma, martingales, Weiner processes, discrete processes
- **Numerical techniques:** Trees, finite differences, Monte Carlo simulation, integration

While it is more of a tool than a concept, MS Excel is critical for productivity in almost every role that a quant would ever consider. I highly recommend two books by John Walkenbach: *The Excel Bible* and *Power Programming with VBA*. While they may look intimidating at 500+ pages each, they are actually very quick and easy reads.

For those who would like to get exposure to the C++ language (from scratch), I found Ivor Horton's Beginning Visual C++ was a very good tool to learn the language (though I am not a programmer at heart, so take this advice with a pinch of salt). Java might be a useful language as well but do not go overboard. Programming aptitude and experience is generally required, but not necessarily in any given language. IT and quant groups often make their new joiners attend seminars or training programs for this sort of thing.

5.2.2 Quantitative Roles

We now go through each of the roles that we assigned a score of 4 or 5 to in terms of quantitative ability. We have also labeled some sub-roles within these previously described roles so that we can better distinguish between them as well. While we described these roles in the last chapter, we now focus on the quantitative areas within the roles. As a result, we are naturally leaving out many other facets that each of the roles entail. It is simply not possible to highlight all possible mathematical aspects of each role, so we have chosen a representative subset.

Analytics: This is the only area I gave a rating of 5 to in terms of quantitative abilities. Analytics teams could be considered as a centralized quantitative resource. They can get involved with virtually any project where quantitative insights are required, but the bulk of their focus revolves around derivatives pricing, hedging, and risk management models.

Working on derivatives models that firms use to price and risk manage billions of dollars worth of transactions is clearly a function that is critical to the success of any derivatives operation. As we discussed before, the nature of the models requires advanced quantitative skills. Stochastic calculus and differential equations are a given for most all quants in this area. This does not mean just a grasp of textbook definitions, but a working knowledge that can easily understand and perhaps contribute to new models and modeling approaches.

Correlation and other portfolio concepts are regularly used within derivatives modeling (CDO and related products being the best example) but also for other portfolio applications such as loan portfolios and risk management. Accordingly, a strong understanding of multivariate distributions and correlation structures (eg, base correlations, copulas, etc) are highly desirable skills.

In terms of implementing and enhancing such models, a strong grasp of numerical methods and programming skills are useful and often a requirement. Classes in both areas are often required for advanced technical degrees. For those looking into this profession, it would be wise to integrate such courses into your curriculum or make a solid effort to learn them on your own.

In terms of which quantitative skills are required, the answer is "all of the above". Basic mathematical and statistical concepts will be assumed. Areas such as stochastic calculus and differential equations (all types) are so widely used that they might as well be assumed mandatory too.

There are several books and resources on the web that are focused on these careers. Paul Wilmott's website (www.wilmott.com) is perhaps the best such tool. It provides a broad spectrum of discussion forums and job postings mostly focused on these types of quant careers.

Flow derivatives trader: We separate flow derivatives trading into two areas: those that deal in vanilla options and the rest that do not. The latter group will generally trade delta-one derivatives or swaps[49], both of which employ relatively simple but often tedious mathematics. Accordingly, we focus on the former as these roles require a slightly higher level of mathematical sophistication.

Options traders, as we explain in *Appendix B: Four Very Common Derivatives*, convert their option positions into volatility exposures through delta-hedging and focus primarily on the implied and realized volatility. They should still have a strong fundamental grasp on the underlying so that they are aware of any potential risks that could significantly move price, be it a stock, bond, commodity, or other asset.

It is probably fair to label flow options traders as volatility traders. In addition to volatility, options traders also monitor a variety of other second order factors that could affect their options prices. Interest rates and dividend assumptions are two such examples. Interest rates can easily be hedged by taking offsetting positions in bonds, (interest rate) swaps or futures. Dividends, however, are not as easily hedged an often require the trader to make an assumption in his pricing calculations.

Second guessing models is also part of an options trader's job. Sometimes the market prices things differently than models do or clients will continue to sell or buy particular options which may make the trader wonder if the market

---

49   Note that interest rate swaps require the same simple mathematics as bonds. Other types of swaps (eg, equity and commodity) basically trade the underlying against other delta-one products according to which are relatively under or over priced.

knows something they do not. Ultimately, the trader must reconcile whether their model or the market is more likely to be right and act accordingly.

As we mentioned before, traders use volatility surfaces to complement (fix) the Black-Scholes framework. These are generally three-dimensional surfaces where a two-dimensional grid is created by the different strikes and maturities of the options, and the third axis indicates the implied volatility for options with those strikes and maturities. Sometimes the underlying asset itself has a maturity dimension of its own (eg, bonds) which require a hyper-surface to maintain the volatility profile for such assets.

At the portfolio level, flow derivative traders will utilize risk management systems to aggregate their risks. The greek sensitivities we discussed before serve as the primary tool to aggregate risks. For example, the implied volatility exposure might be summed up by netting all of the vegas across the portfolio. This netting will usually involve some adjustments (eg, weighting) to account for different option maturities (ie, the vega of a five year option poses different risks than the vega of a three month option).

Given that netting risks via the greeks ignores many other aspects, risk is assessed via other relevant factors as well. Any one portfolio could have significant exposures to sectors, regions, or specific assets. It is normally preferred not to have any *concentration risk* unless the trader is intentionally speculating on that factor (eg, the trader believes volatility will go up in Russia and has significant long vega positions in the region).

So the mathematics behind most options trading is effectively the same as for options pricing models and risk management. This amounts to a firm grasp of the Black-Scholes framework and some of the common enhancements to the model. Furthermore, intimate familiarity of calculus and mathematical derivatives is an absolute requirement since it is the foundation for risk management (ie, the greeks).

Exotic derivatives trader: Here we are referring to those who trade non-vanilla derivative products such as those required for structured products. Mathematically speaking, one might characterize exotic products as those which are not in the *linear span* of vanilla derivatives. If a product could be broken down into vanilla components, the flow derivatives traders could handle them.

A typical example of a structured product would be a call option on the performance of an equally weighted basket of, say, the S&P 500, FTSE 100, Euro STOXX 50, and Nikkei 225 indices. While there are vanilla options available on each of the individual indices, there is not combination of them that can replicate the option on the basket. On might use a basket of those options to hedge, but there is a residual correlation exposure (exactly as we discussed above in the context of dispersion trades). This type of hedging is widely used by exotics and other correlation traders. Packages with an *option on a basket* together with a *basket of options* have become known as OBBOs.

Given the complexity of these products, exotics traders naturally require more sophisticated pricing, hedging, and risk management models. This market is primarily traded OTC and data is sparse at best. As a result, exotics desks work very closely with Analytics teams who focus on such models. When possible, the exotics traders share real market data on exotic products with the Analytics teams so they can use it to test and enhance their models.

Another byproduct of the inherent complexity is the margins that get integrated into the pricing. Trading such products involves more risks and exotics traders increase their prices (lower if they are buying) to compensate for potential losses associated with those risks. However, as models improve and competition increases, margins will continue to get squeezed. Notwithstanding, part of the reason structuring teams exist is so that they can use their innovation to create new products and embed more profit margin.

The basket option above is just a simple example; many products are much more complex. Even those that appear simple in terms of their payout often require sophisticated hedging considerations. The management of the risks is more complicated with exotics derivates that with flow derivatives. While exotics traders monitor all of the typical greeks as described above, they must also consider others in order to analyze their risks properly. As we pointed out, correlation is one such risk, but there are many others that measure the changes in one greek relative to another. Mathematically speaking, these *cross-term* risks are mixed partial derivatives and they often get interesting labels like volga, vanna, vomma, zomma, etc.

Just as with flow traders, exotic risks are aggregated so that they can be analyzed at the portfolio level. The cross-term risks make risk management more complicated. For example, second order risks can be more significant and must be accounted for during a stress test[50]. More fundamental risk factors such as sector and regional exposures are highlighted as well.

Credit products such as CDOs (please see *Appendix C: The Collateralized Debt Obligation (CDO)* for a description of this product) are very exotic. The transformation of the risks into tranches dramatically increases the complexity of this product, especially with regard to pricing and hedging. Accordingly, these products are managed by exotic trading desks. While greek risks are monitored for CDOs, portfolio dynamics and loss distributions are the key focus and require extensive modeling and risk management tools.

Exotics traders do not necessarily possess the same quantitative sophistication as their colleagues in Analytics but they still must be able to grasp many of the same concepts in terms of the risk management and modeling. In addition, they must be familiar with the mechanics of pricing and hedging models so that they can work together with their Analytics colleagues to improve their models. One might say that exotics traders need a deeper understanding of the same concepts that flow derivatives traders must be familiar with.

Proprietary trader / Junior PM / Buy-side researcher / Quantitative (Sell-side) Researcher:

The level of quantitative skills varies amongst these different roles depending upon the asset class, strategies, and amount of derivatives involved. To the extent that any of these roles focus on derivatives, they will require the skills described just above. While these are all very different roles, here we focus on several different quantitative areas that are commonly used within all of them.

The first notion we discuss is *back-testing*. Researchers and traders will often conceive different ideas for trading strategies or integrating various types of information into their decision making process. As the cliché phrase stipulates, "past performance is not necessarily indicative of future returns". Even so, it is often revealing to know how different ideas would have translated into profits or losses. Accordingly, many analysts (whatever their specific role, be

---

50   A stress test is a practice used by risk management teams that involves changing the value of one or more underlyings and assessing the impact on a portfolio's value.

it trading, research, etc) acquire historical data to investigate whether these ideas have merit.

A typical example might be to look at whether or not the shape of the yield curve has any predictive ability for the equity markets. First, one must quantify the "shape of the yield curve", perhaps taking the spread between the one month and one year interest rates as the metric to observe. Then one can measure the subsequent, say, one month, performance of the relevant equity market at each point in time. Once this data is in place, one can compute the average equity returns for different shapes of the rate curve. Figure 19 below provides a generic illustration of what these results might look like. In this (made up) example, steeper interest rate curves appear to have precipitated equity market declines. It is worth noting that this is just one simple way to go about this analysis; there are many alternative approaches.

Figure 19: Generic Back-Test Results

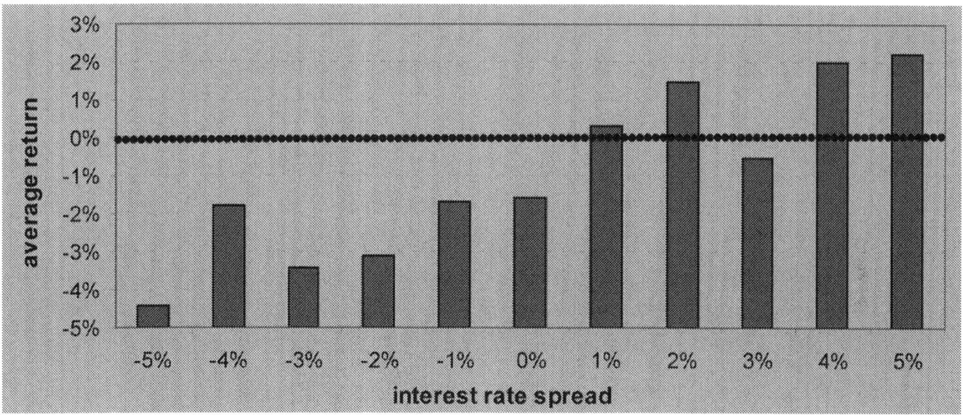

While the signal above was as simple observable number (interest rate spread), sometimes signals are not easily observable or require extensive calculations (eg, regressions or even neural networks). Additionally, the assets whose behavior is being observed are not always as easy as equity markets to track (volatility or credit default swaps for example) or require additional manipulations of data. As evidenced here, back-testing can vary in its mathematical complexity from simple if/then statements to artificially intelligent algorithms. Regressions, however, seem to take the cake for the most widely used (and abused) back-testing tool within financial markets.

Another area of related research is *cross asset class* modeling. Using information in one asset class to help make decisions in another, or possibly trade them against each other (ie, relative value), has been a wildly popular idea in recent years. Notwithstanding, the degree of success it has achieved is questionable.

The *Merton model* is probably the most popular and best example of cross asset class research. It describes another elegant mathematical relationship between the credit (ie, probability of default) of a company and its equity (ie, stock price). Instead of modeling either one directly, it models the assets of the company as a stochastic process and derives the value of both as contingent claims (ie, options) on these assets. This model is one of many that have been used to model debt-equity relationships which generally fall under the heading of *capital structure* models.

Another tool often used to capture the behavior of assets and predict their future directions is *time series* analysis. Time series models often have names like ARMA and ARCH[51]. Time series analysis is essentially a statistical discipline that seeks to identify temporal relationships between data points in a numerical sequence (ie, how past data influences or relates to later data). As such, it is often applied to asset prices and other related quantities (eg, interest rates). In this author's opinion, time series is overused and often abused tool.

The last area we highlight for these roles is portfolio analysis; investors are always interested in how to achieve higher returns or lower risk in their portfolios. The strategies used to analyze this can vary as we discussed before. One can use a simple approach that requires only basic statistics or something more complex that involves non-linear optimizations to analyze their portfolios.

Given the different types of applications we just discussed, one can see that these types of roles vary greatly in focus and the degree of required quantitative sophistication. The mathematics can range from simple logic to stochastic processes or optimization, for example. As a result, it is critical for candidates to understand what any one role entails in order to assess the required quantitative skill sets.

Structurer: The quantitative sophistication of most structuring units is probably one notch lower than those of exotics, which is one or more notches

---

51   ARMA = autoregressive moving average and ARCH = autoregressive conditional heteroskedasticity.

lower than Analytics. While they must often liaise with exotics traders about the products they construct, structurers usually do not need to understand the risks as thoroughly as the traders. The more technical issues are usually tackled by the Analytics or exotics trading teams, so the quantitative requirements for structurers are not as high.

Most conversations structurers have with traders will not include intricate details such as those related to the models, but more superficial topics such as the payout structures. Structurers will often price the products they are working on using internal tools. They will have to understand the models to the extent that they have to choose different models and parameters to price different products.

Structurers also carry out much back-testing. Back-tests have become an essential tool for marketing many of their products. In fact, there are hardly any presentations that present products without an accompanying back-test chart that amounts to a squiggly line pointing north (ie, the product would have made money historically has this idea been employed).

One potential exception to this description is the credit structuring desk. Credit structuring inherently requires more sophistication because of the types of products they deal with (eg, CDOs). Moreover, many of these credit structuring desks have their own Analytics personnel within their team. While these business units might be labeled as structuring, the quantitative sophistication can be on par with that of the Analytics team for some roles.

Risk research: Most risk managers are focused on monitoring risk, but some banks employ a risk research team to develop the methodologies to analyze and calculate risk. They are also often responsible for *model validation* when new models are proposed for business use.

Measuring risk is a broad topic. *Value at risk* is often a core focus and it requires basic statistical concepts once a loss distribution is in place. However, risk methodologies are often focused on the aggregation of risks so that a combined loss distribution can be generated. Just as with individual trading positions, complex relationships exist between different businesses. It is generally the case that most businesses are positively correlated. Indeed, few businesses do not suffer, let alone perform well, in market downturns.

As a result, risk methodologies often deal with joint distributions and correlations when combining different sources of risks. They will also employ historical or Monte Carlo simulations to generate loss distributions. Conditional expectations and other statistical concepts are also used in risk research, sometime in the context of assessing tail risks[52] and value at risk.

Risk research teams are normally charged with the task of validating new models that the business units want to use; this provides a system of checks and balances. Naturally some models are more complex than others, so risk researchers must be sufficiently competent to deal with many types of models. As a result, risk research groups often require a thorough knowledge of derivatives and the underlying models so that they can assess new and related models.

On balance, the quantitative skills required for risk research are not on par with Analytics teams. However, they are also broad in scope and require solid understanding across several quantitative areas. Basic statistical concepts should be a given, but an advanced understanding of how to aggregate risks and the related correlation structures is also necessary, as is a solid grasp of derivatives modeling.

---

52   Tail risks are risks that have a low probability of occurring.

Little nuggets you might be able to use to impress interviewers

* Use them at your discretion as some interviewers might interrogate your comments!

- "We are so lucky to have the exponential function in finance. Otherwise, many of our closed form formulas would explode or not even be possible with all of the unwieldy interest rate calculations."
- "The book definition of gamma (how much delta changes etc…) is not practical. It really describes the exposure of an option position to realized volatility."
- "Option pricing models still do not account for skew or term structure of volatility; volatility surfaces are really just bandages to an imperfect model."
- "Risk as measured by volatility is at odds with asset pricing models since, all else equal, lower prices effectively reduce risk since you are buying things cheaper."
- "Correlation really is an elegant statistic -1, 0, +1 corresponding to specific cases; but it is biased towards larger magnitude observations."
- "It is amazing there are so many companies and so much analysis based on efficient frontiers based on backward looking volatility, return, and correlation figures."
- "It seems to me that the financial community abuses the term arbitrage too much (eg, risk arb?!). Are there really any *arbitrage* profits to be made?"
- "It seems curious that there are so many derivative models based on the notion of independent increments, but at the same time so much time-series analysis which challenges those assumptions."
- "Knowing that *at-the-money* option prices are almost linear in terms of implied volatility can be very helpful when making approximations."

Chapter 5 Concepts

- Definition of a quant
- Theory vs practice for modeling
- Bond math / DCF analyses
- Risk premium
- Quantitative equity modeling
- Technical analysis
- Efficient frontier
- Transition matrices
- Value at risk (V@R)
- No arbitrage principle
- Risk neutral pricing
- Black-Scholes framework
- The greeks and delta hedging
- Delta-one products
- Volatility arbitrage
- Dispersion
- Concentration risk and stress tests
- Exotic derivatives
- Back-testing
- Cross asset class modeling
- Quantitative roles

Chapter 6:

Tips and Insights

The following is broken into two primary sections followed by a third which lists recommended reading and websites. The first section covers a variety of topics related to finding and landing a job that is good for you. The second covers a variety of topics related to issues one encounters on the job. The primary goal of these sections is to help the reader become aware of how things operate from "the other side" at each stage. Understanding the policies and processes that dictate the actions of employers is essential to being better prepared for success in finding, getting, and succeeding in a suitable role.

6.1 Landing the Right Job

This section discusses a variety of topics and strategies for identifying and landing a good job. Before delving into these topics specifically, the first section focuses on internships as we find them to be an invaluable tool for candidates to get experience and increase their chances of landing permanent positions down the road.

6.1.1 Internships

As just mentioned, we cannot emphasize enough how invaluable *internships* can be to the process of looking for permanent jobs down the road. For clarity, we define an internship as essentially a summer job – though some are often structured to take place during a fall or winter school semesters – where there are no commitments on your or the employer's behalf beyond those few months.

Firstly, you can earn some extra money; that never hurts. More importantly, you will be gaining experience while getting an inside look at the industry. This also provides you with an opportunity to start building network of contacts which can be invaluable. A well regarded feature on the resume, an internship not only shows initiative, but can also indicate a real interest in the industry if the internship is related to jobs you are looking for down the road.

Internships can serve as fast tracks into an industry; they are generally easier to get as the bar is lower for hiring. Banks and other institutions often regard internships as three month interviews and thus do not screen candidates as rigorously as they would those applying for permanent positions. The firms have no further obligations but they will often extend (permanent) job offers to candidates who do well as interns.

> **Quick comment:** If it is not too late, run out and get one before you graduate. In fact, fill as many summers as you can with internships as the benefits are invaluable.

6.1.2 Why do Firms so Often Require PhDs and Ivy League Educations?

One thing that can be frustrating for non-PhDs is that many roles list a PhD as a requirement and will not accept applications from anyone who does not have one. Many firms prefer to hire candidates with PhDs for roles that seemingly do not require them. Indeed, most of the roles and activities that we discussed in Chapter 5 generally only require quantitative skills up to and including those with a score of 4; I only gave a score of 5 to one area (analytics).

I have found that there are two primary reasons for this PhD focus. The first is that firms want to make sure that candidates they hire can do the jobs. Even if 90% of roles that employ quants do not actually require a PhD level education, firms still often hire PhDs. They do this to be absolutely sure because the consequences of making a bad hiring decision are difficult to deal with; firing or transferring employees involves an enormous amount of effort and liability. This same notion applies to employers considering candidates with master's degrees versus bachelor's degrees.

The other, and perhaps more important, reason for hiring PhDs is that this degree means the candidates have conducted independent research and written it up in the form of a dissertation. PhDs have demonstrated they are capable of working independently and this is a very desirable trait for most roles. While independent research or a dissertation is often required for other degrees (eg, master's), it is not always the case; a PhD guarantees this is the case. And this is the bottom line: PhDs are a distinguishing feature that make it easier for employers to categorize and screen candidates. Even if you are smarter and more capable than many of the people who have PhDs, and you are capable to doing one, you simply have not proven it and you cannot expect firms to consider you on equal footing.

The same notion applies to educational backgrounds. Many firms clearly perceive some universities as more prestigious than others and they screen job applications accordingly. There are often many applications and those filtering through resumes (initially it will likely be someone in HR) will be afforded the liberty of setting high standards. Given that Ivy League institutions seem to produce better candidates on average, employers will use educational backgrounds to screen candidates. Moreover, this implicitly leverages the presumably more rigorous admissions processes used by these universities. These practices do not always mean that any of these candidates are necessarily better for any given job, but all else equal, it does it does give them better odds when it comes to consideration.

However, all else is not always equal. The strategies we discuss in this chapter are geared to help everyone, regardless of type or level of education, increase their chances of finding and landing a job in financial services. While some of these are simply tweaks to the normal application process, other informal tactics such as networking and courteous follow-up (be careful not to harass potential employers!) can greatly improve your odds versus other candidates who do not employ them.

6.1.3 The Job Search

Given that you are reading this book, it is likely that you are interested in working in the financial services industry. However, as the previous chapters make clear, the spectrum of potential roles in this industry is very broad and will require you to give significant thought to how you can narrow your search. As you start your job search, you should come up with a list of criteria or questions that relate to the different roles you will investigate. Some of these might include:

- Are you qualified?
- Does it pay well?
- Is the role compatible with my personality?
- Are the hours compatible with the lifestyle I desire?
- Is the location OK? The commute?

- Will you be able to apply what you have studied?
- Is the role challenging enough?
- Is it dynamic enough?
- Will you maintain a steep learning curve?
- Will I have enough responsibility or input into the organization?
- Would I be happy working with these people?

The previous five chapters were meant to familiarize you with the industry and the different roles within, culminating in Chapter 4 and Chapter 5 which were meant to help out in this area by assessing your compatibility with more specific roles. But by no means do they detail all of the different possible aspects of all jobs. You will have to decide which factors are most important to yourself and judge accordingly. After looking around and seeing the jobs that are available, you will almost surely have to compromise on some aspects and perhaps even reevaluate your criteria. If I can stress only one thing, as generic or cliché as it may sound, you should do your absolute best to find a job that you think you will enjoy (or at very least not despise!).

Given your level of ambition or desperation, you may choose to spread the net narrower or wider. Many of us are eager just to get in the door, anywhere, while others are focused on a specific role (eg, "I want to be a trader" rings a bell). You will have to use your own judgment in what strategy you choose. At the risk of stating the obvious, spreading the net too narrow may reduce the number of opportunities you consider and the chances of landing a job. However, spreading the net too wide may create confusion or send mixed signals to the employers with whom you are applying. For example, if a candidate claims they would like to work in sales *or* trading, there are two possible conclusions an interviewer will draw; either the client does not know enough to pick between these two incredibly different roles or he is so desperate he is looking for anything. Accordingly, even if you do choose to spread the net very wide, it is in your best interests not to let on that you did.

So where to start? The good news is that most large firms have websites that make applying for jobs with them a fairly straightforward process. They often post job openings, though these are generally for more experienced roles. Firms also have recruiting programs focused on finding recent graduates. They even go as far as to visit campuses and job fairs to reach out to and find candidates.

If you feel that you would like to look more broadly than the list of companies you might have come up with, you can also look at websites such as www.monster.com[53] or www.efinancialcareers.com where thousands of job openings are listed from many different employers. These websites are oriented towards more experienced positions but it can give you an idea of other potential employers even if you do not find many suitable roles for yourself.

The bad news is that you will be one of thousands (perhaps tens of thousands) who will be submitting applications. Once you submit your application, you might feel ignorant and helpless as you have no idea where it has ended up or what is being done with it. You are of course entitled to follow up, call human resource departments, and ask about the status of your application, but that is likely to get a generic response.

You should, however, consider following up in another manner to help shift the odds more in your favor. In particular, you should use whatever means necessary to find internal contacts and follow up with them. By internal contacts we are referring to employees of the firms you are applying to who work in or near the area(s) you are considering. This may sound like a formidable task, but it is more a question of effort than difficulty. One cannot overstate the importance of having internal contacts that can vouch for you when it comes to getting your application past the initial screening stages and beyond.

There are two natural sources you should be able to leverage without much difficulty. The first obvious resource at your disposal for this is your friends and family. Chances are that either they, or someone they know, will know people that work at the firms you are interested in. The other natural source of help for this effort will come from people related to your university or college (and of course your fraternity or sorority if you were in one).

Most large schools will have a department dedicated to helping its students find jobs. While this may not necessarily facilitate your networking effort, it may help out in other ways (eg, resumes, interviewing techniques, etc). You should also reach out to your professors and leverage contacts or recommendations they may be able to share with you.

---

53   Please note that this website lists jobs of all types, both within and outside financial services.

Your fellow alumni are also a good source for networking, though they may prove difficult to track down. If your university does not maintain records to track alumni, or they cannot share them with you, there is another source that can do this quite easily: Bloomberg (not the mayor of New York but the flagship product of his company[54]). The business school at your university (if it exists) might have a Bloomberg terminal available for you to use. If not, you might have to ask a friend in the financial industry who has one. However you are able to access it, use the PEOP function on Bloomberg to help track down any fellow alumni that are also on the Bloomberg system. Not only does this function identify where they work, but it also provides contact details[55].

For those of you who are comfortable cold calling and speaking with people you do not know, you can also use what might be called the scuttlebutt method. Here you would proactively identify and list relevant industry persons who appear in papers (eg, Barron's, the Wall Street Journal, etc), magazines (eg, Risk or Institutional Investor[56]), and on television (eg, CNBC or Bloomberg). The earlier you start your list, the more comprehensive it will be when you are ready to start following up on the leads. While this is likely to lead to many dead ends, it could take just one person who recognized and appreciated your initiative to open a door for you.

If you are not comfortable with the above approaches or they do not work for you, you can always enlist the help of a headhunter. There are many such firms out there. They generally prefer experienced hires but many cater to juniors as well. Analytic Recruiting, Michael Paige, Orgtel, Huxley, and Selby Jennings are some examples, but please see the table of *recommended resources* at the end of this chapter for an overview of job related websites.

---

54   Bloomberg is an expensive software package that is widely used by the financial services industry as a source of news, data and related tools. It was started by Michael Bloomberg, the current Mayor of New York City.

55   FYI - if you dial the main contact number for most firms, they will connect to anyone you ask for.

56   The most relevant types of magazines like these are not generally found on the shelves. Instead, they require costly subscriptions. University business departments often maintain such subscriptions but the magazines also maintain websites that could be useful.

6.1.4 Applying: Resume, Cover Letter, and Following Up

The basic application process is generally straightforward; most firms will ask you to submit a resume and a cover letter. Some firms will require you to type the information directly into their website, others will ask for you to simply submit the resume and cover letter as Microsoft Word or Adobe PDF documents.

In any case, it is in your best interest to create an electronic resume and cover letter. In fact, it may be helpful to do more than one of each if time permits. No two jobs or employers are the same. Accordingly, it can work to your advantage to tailor both your cover letter and your resume to each role for which you apply, highlighting any pertinent experience. If you have done an internship, this is a prime area you can tweak.

If you are just starting your career, your resume will primarily reflect your educational background and it may be difficult to tailor. In any case, you do not want to change too much. First, you do not want to be untruthful. But second, you can lose track of what you have told different potential employers. If you do some tweaking, you should keep copies of each version and be sure to review what you have sent people/firms before each communication with them. In the end, you will have to balance what you have time to do and what you are comfortable doing.

When you are preparing a resume, you should assume that it will only be skimmed over when it is first submitted; it will not be read in its entirety. Accordingly, you should make sure your resume is presentable, well organized, and highlights the areas which you want to standout.

In terms of the content, be as concise as possible. It is only polite given that the people looking at your resume will also be looking at 10s, 100s, or possibly 1,000s of others. You also do not want to stretch the truth too far on your resume. While you want to give yourself the highest chance of making it past each stage of screening, one of the absolute worst things that can happen is to be caught in a lie. We list a few suggestions that should help you accomplish this:

- Make sure your name is prominent and at the top, perhaps in a larger or bold font
- Include your contact details just below: phone number(s) and email are sufficient but some people like to include their address
- Educational background in reverse chronological order. Do not go back to kindergarten; they usually start with university or college
- Work experience, if any[57]. Include the firm or institution name, start and end dates, and geography if it is not obvious (but be consistent throughout)
- Awards/affiliations: Any recognition of your achievements or honor societies, business clubs, etc that you participated in
- Interests and hobbies: Mostly to show that you are not a hermit, but also for the slight chance that you will have something in common with someone who reads your resume. Nothing too personal or too far off the beaten path. Be cautious. Quirky may be ok but not include anything too weird. Do not include Playstation, Wii, etc

While it is not necessarily critical for you to customize your resumes for each job you apply for, it is important that you tailor your cover letters. Indeed, the purpose of a cover letter is to explain why you are interested in a particular position and why you are the best person to for it. Accordingly, you should do some research on each company you are applying to. Once you have a better grasp on company's culture and business focus, specifically the area(s) you are applying to, you can present yourself and your qualifications so that you target the role(s) in question. In particular, you should attempt to make at least one concrete connection between a specific aspect of the firm and yourself. Explain how a specific project or endeavor that you were involved with relates to a specific aspect of their business and how your experience could prove useful. This could be a school project, entrepreneurial venture, or experience from an internship, for example. However, think hard about what examples you choose and make sure that they are indeed related.

Another characteristic that employers desire in candidates is their ability to start and complete projects, both alone and in a team setting. You want to show that you are not just book smart, but that you are capable of tackling real projects and seeing them through. You can do this on your resume, cover letter, or both. Even if you do not include something like this on your resume

---

57   If you have significant work experience, this should be placed before education. The goal is to place the most important aspects closer to the top.

or cover letter, there is a 99% chance that you will be asked about a project that you worked on and had significant input. While you can elaborate in your cover letter, you will have to be more concise in the resume. You might want to consider using phrases such as "Built XYZ from scratch", "conceived and implemented XYZ", "brought XYZ to fruition", etc. In any case, you should make it clear that you can successfully start and finish tasks and projects, perhaps even in high pressure situations.

In addition to the recommendations above concerning resumes and cover letters, we also suggest that you add a personal touch outside of formal process of submitting these documents. You can do this both before and after you submit for application. In particular, we suggest you participate in as many job fairs and recruiting events as possible. Just as we stressed the importance of having an internal contact, meeting people in person should only help your cause. Just by meeting someone and shaking their hand, you will have made an impression and planted yourself in their mind. Naturally, it is in your best interests to make good impressions that will stick.

As we previously mentioned, you may begin to feel a bit powerless after you submit your formal application as you will have no idea as to whether your submission went into some electronic abyss or is being read by the manager of a role that you would really like. Human resources generally will not give you any more information than is posted on their website, except possibly whether things look to be going according to schedule or not.

In any case, you should be tactful and certainly not harass anyone. There is a delicate balance between being persistent and annoying. This is where your internal contacts can be very useful. Depending upon how close you are, you might be able to get them to make sure your resume does not get lost in the process. They might be able to inquire with human resources to track your application, or help it get through. At very least you will help yourself to stand out and make your name more noticeable if anyone comes across it on an application, resume or cover letter. Again, exercise caution in your approach as most people in this business (and human resources) are likely to be very busy and you are not likely to be a priority.

6.1.5 Group Assessment Programs

Some firms bring in hordes of graduates all at once and make them participate in a variety of team and individual tasks or tests. If you participate in such an event, you should understand that they are looking for those individuals that standout, but for good reason.

The group or team exercises are generally designed to identify leadership qualities and team working skills. You will be working with a handful of other people to achieve a common goal. Being a wallflower, speaking only when spoken to, is not good. Neither is completely dominating the entire exercise. You want to be able to show that you can think intelligently on your feet, make valuable contributions to the efforts, and perhaps even lead or motivate others to do so.

Coupled with this group exercises will be individual exercises (not including interviews) which are designed to test aptitude, regardless of educational background. So preparing for these is a bit like preparing for any standardized test. You might want to brush up on different topics, perhaps focus on those you are not particular fresh or comfortable with. Notwithstanding, there is a strong bias for these tests to revolve around mathematical or analytics topics.

6.1.6 Interviewing

Before you have any interview, you should do your homework. Find out as much about the firm, the role and possibly even the people you will be interviewing with. You do not have to know everything. At the junior level, you are generally not expected to know much, if anything, about the industry unless you are coming from a finance or MBA related background. But you want to at least have some explanation as to why you are there interviewing with that specific firm or role.

Once it comes to interview time you should do your best to relax. Being nervous or anxious is not uncommon, some people even sweat, but these things can really only work against you. Firstly, you might not be able to think clearly if you are not comfortable. Worse yet, you will not be making a good impression as interviewers naturally prefer those who are not nervous and can remain calm under pressure. Indeed, no interviewer likes to start things off shaking hands with somebody who has sweaty palms[58].

---

58   Speaking of handshakes, one thing you want to make sure you do not have is a "dead fish" handshake. A limp handshake can attach a stigma of feebleness or lack of confidence. I suggest a natural handshake with a pulse of firmness. Not too strong, but definitely not limp. Keep in mind that you do not want it to appear premeditated, but natural and without any thought.

One strategy to help you relax before interviews is to allow yourself some extra time and go to a nearby café for half an hour before you are due to arrive. Do not try to cram the morning's Wall Street Journal or Financial Times into your head. Instead, bring some leisure reading that will help get your mind off of the process.

It is critically important you try to manage your time so that you are not rushed or hurried. Running late or even close to it can only bring about more undue stress. Obviously, showing up late is clearly a bad sign to your interviewer and cuts into the time you have to interview. If there is even a remote chance that you may be late, you should do your best to forewarn human resources or the interviewer as early as possible. This could be the day of the interview or earlier if you know that there is some reason you could be late (eg, you have a test or another interview beforehand).

During the interview, the interviewer will likely ask you a series of questions. You should be sure you understand the questions and that your answers are pertinent. If you do not know the answer or what the interviewer is referring to, it is usually best to state so. Rattling off an irrelevant answer will not win you any points. Try to present your answers and communications in a confident, but not arrogant fashion. Rational, thought out responses can score well even when you are not entirely correct.

Another thing to keep in mind is that interviews are two-way processes: The firm is interviewing you for a position, but you are also interviewing the firm. Make absolutely sure that you have a list of questions that you can ask various interviewers. Depending upon the flow of the interview, you may want to ask your questions along the way or reserve them for the last few minutes. Some examples of questions could be:

- What sets your firm's [insert specific business unit] business apart from other firms?
- In what ways is your firm's culture conducive to promoting meritocracy?
- What is a typical day like in your business?
- What career tracks are possible for this role?
- Do all new joiners attend a training program?

Last, but certainly not least, you will almost certainly run into some analytical questions or brainteasers, many of which will be completely irrelevant to finance. If you are applying for a quantitative role, some of these questions will test specific topics from your mathematics educational (eg, please perform this integral, derive the Black-Scholes formula, etc). However, other questions will not require any specific education. They will be testing your aptitude and your ability to think under pressure.

In either case, you should make sure you understand the question clearly; regurgitate it if necessary. Do not get stressed even if you do not know the answer. Your reaction and thought process are more important than the final answer. So explain and be clear about your logical thinking. There are numerous books and internet websites dedicated to these types of questions. These resources essentially defeat the purpose of testing analytical thinking, but I suspect most people go through as many as they can to get an edge.

Many of these questions are based on a handful of quantitative foundations (eg, expectations, Newtonian and stochastic calculus, etc), but logical reasoning is probably the most common. Your best bet is to GOOGLE things like "brain teasers investment banking interviews" or check out books like Timothy Falcon's "Heard on the Street". Getting a grip on these types of questions is imperative not just for quants but almost all candidates.

Lastly, one thing that seems to be taboo for junior candidates to bring up is compensation. Do not discuss this unless someone specifically brings it up with you. But this is highly unlikely. Indeed, it is mostly irrelevant for junior level hires at most firms as standard packages are the norm. Should you receive one, this type of information will be completely covered in any offer letter.

6.1.7 Getting and Weighing Up Offers

While you may have interviewed well, convinced employers that you are better than other candidates, and made them want to have you onboard, it is possible that they do not extend you an offer. As strange as that sounds, there is a larger process taking place of which you are a small part; understanding the logic behind the process can make all the difference.

For starters, there is a fairly well defined limit on the number of jobs that a firm is trying to fill with candidates from any one recruiting class. Naturally, not every offer will be accepted, so they sometimes make more offers than they have jobs. However, if they offer too many more than they actually have room for, then could end up hiring more than they need or can accommodate.

One specific problem with the selection process is that higher quality candidates generally receive multiple offers from different firms, thereby decreasing the likeliness of accepting of any particular offer. One strategy to tackle this issue is to put in some extra effort to make that candidate feel special. This could be as little as an extra phone call to shower a little more praise and highlight the upside to the role they are offering. They might even invite them into the office to spend a morning or afternoon. Or they might wine and dine the candidate for an extra special touch.

This special treatment is generally reserved only for a small fraction of exceptional candidates that the firm identifies and is willing to invest more time and effort to recruit. For the broader pool of candidates, they employ another strategy as well. Indeed, once they have crossed off candidates they do not like and narrowed their search down to a smaller group of quality candidates, they will begin to rank them. This ranking will include the obvious criteria around abilities, communication skills, etc, but also the likeliness of accepting an offer. For avoidance of doubt, they will prefer candidates that are more likely to accept their offer, all else equal.

As a result, candidates can use this bias to their advantage. This is not to say that you should declare outright that you will unequivocally accept any offer that they give you. Indeed, this reeks of desperation and will more likely raise an eyebrow than catalyze an offer. Instead, a better approach might be to first let them know you do have other offers and/or that you are following up on some other opportunities. This is to be expected and can also make you look more attractive to them as they will note that other firms have identified you as a quality candidate. However, the key is for you to let them know that you are specifically interviewing with them because you prefer some facets of their firm in particular. This could be the culture of the firm, a particular business they excel at, or someone you know who is happy working there. The goal here is to sincerely (but subtly as to not sound premeditated) convey that you are likely to accept an offer from them.

While not worthless, verbal offers are not nearly as valuable as they would be in writing. Nonetheless, many firms will give out verbal offers. They have little downside in doing so and in some cases are feeling candidates out to see if they would accept. Whatever you do, do not make decisions based on verbal offers; get it in writing.

Once you have it in writing, you always have the option to take an offer until it expires; it is contractual[59]. Do not cut yourself short based on pressure from any firm or manager following up on their offer. Use your intuition in weighing other potential opportunities against offers that you already have. Always make absolutely sure you have signed contracts and are ready to go with another firm before turning down any other firms' offers.

Sometimes you might find yourself interviewing for jobs even after you have offers for other jobs you think you might prefer. In this case, you might be tempted to forego the rest of the interviewing, but this can be a mistake. The experience can only help you as long as you do not miss any other offers' deadlines and it is always in your best interest to get as much information as possible. Indeed, you might change your mind about which job is best for you. Ideally, all of these processes would occur at the same time and there would be no timing issues, but this is rarely the case.

Quick comment: When you are choosing your first job, you are making one of the biggest decisions in your life. Unfortunately, you also have the least relevant experience to make an informed decision at this time. This is just the way it is. The best way for you to prepare is to find out as much about this industry (and related jobs) as you can through various resources including the internet, books, other people, and when possible, interning at a firm in the industry.

6.2 On the Job

6.2.1 Figure Out Your Manager

Some managers like to micro manage and others provide a long leash. It is in your best interest to figure out what your manager's preferred approach is. The onus is really on them to suggest a structure to your communications,

---

59   There have been instances of offers being retracted or postponed, even after they have been accepted. This is usually catalyzed by the firm having major difficulties and having to trim down at all costs. In these cases, there is usually some sort of compensation for breaking the contract.

but it cannot hurt you to observe and conduct yourself as you think your manager would like.

In general, it is safe to assume that your manager is a busy person and that you should not burden him/her with minute details. Try to use your colleagues for getting up to speed and various other details.

6.2.2 Find a Sponsor or Mentor

Many firms operate programs whereby new junior employees are given a mentor or required to find one. Whether this is a formal engagement or not, it is important to have someone senior in the firm looking out for your best interests. This might just be your line manager but sometimes your line manager is not very senior, not very good, or you simply find someone else who believes you have talent and might look out for you. In any case, it is critically important that you find support from some senior level. If your line manager does not turn out to be your mentor, it may take some time to identify one. Naturally, it makes sense to find someone in your general business division. Your work would likely be more visible to someone in the same business and it could help impose an upward gravity on your career. Moreover, if your manager knows that one of his own superiors supports you, he will likely adopt a similar view. These benefits could come in many forms ranging from day to day support, promotion, and pay.

6.2.3 Doing a Good Job is Only the Start

First and foremost, it is only ethical (and productive) for you to put your heart into your work and do a good job. However, there is often a need to not only do a good job, but also to make others aware. Promoting your work and visibly contributing your thoughtful input where possible will be incredibly helpful to raise your profile and credibility. If you have a well intentioned and capable manager, then they will likely promote your work and help make you visible to higher echelons of management. I have been lucky and most of my managers have done just that but I have also observed several instances where this was not the case.

Some managers are insecure or simply not good at managing. They (or your colleagues!) might suppress your contributions and/or attempt to take credit for your work. This is not an easy scenario to deal with, especially when you are very junior. Candidly discussing your manager's flaws with him is probably not a rosy scenario. Worse yet, it is possible that he would then view you as a threat and react by systematically damaging your reputation. Going to human resources, another colleague or manager puts you at risk of being perceived as a rat going behind other people's backs. It is a delicate topic and you should tread carefully as politics cannot be underestimated in these situations.

To close this topic on a high note, we note that most managers are good at their jobs and that is why they are there. Bad managers are generally weeded out of the ranks regularly[60]. But whether it is you, your manager, or your combined efforts, raising your profile based on good work and business input is certainly a fast track to promotion and more responsibility, both of which should be positively correlated with your compensation.

6.2.4 Leverage Other Resources

Many financial professionals have advanced degrees that required them to do independent research. While those skills are useful, it would be wasteful not to make use of the resources that are available to you within the firm. Firstly, you have your colleagues and you should leverage their experience as best you can without becoming an incessant burden. Most large firms employ 100s of people to publish valuable research on economics and various asset classes; you can usually access this for free. These firms often have in house libraries that can loan you (or sometimes acquire if they do not have) copies of commercial and academic publications (eg, magazines, journals, etc) or access a variety of data sources. The point of mentioning all of these resources is to make you aware that they are available for you to leverage in the context of your work; you do not have to do everything yourself.

6.2.5 Politics Cannot be Ignored

While you will be busy with your own workload when you first start, it is incredibly important not to underestimate the politics that are at work on all levels. Not to sound Machiavellian, but many of your fellow new joiners will be jockeying to stand out (in a favorable way) from day one and will not hesitate to use you as a stepping stone. Fast forward several years and it's the same game, just at a higher level.

---

60   Bonus time comes around once a year and is probably the most commonly used tool to deal with underperformers. It is much easier and involves less potential liability when someone chooses to leave the firm after receiving a smaller bonus than they think they deserve.

One cardinal rule to follow (perhaps in any setting?) is to avoid speaking negatively about others. However, if you must, do so only with people you are absolutely certain are *on your side*. You could also take this further and praise others more often, even those you might not think deserve it. Few things will endear you more to others than when they hear that you have spoken favorably about them to others.

The main idea here is to minimize the number of people who dislike or distrust you and maximize the number who do like and trust you. You will have far fewer bullets to dodge as you progress your career, increasing the likelihood of your survival and promotion.

There are, however, a few mavericks that wear their hearts on their sleeves and call a spade a spade when they see one. They will have a well known reputation for calling it as they see it and command deep respect, if not fear, from many of their colleagues. These types of people are often more difficult to deal with and their outspokenness can sometimes put their own manager in awkward positions. Accordingly, these types do not always get the same support from their own manager. This, in conjunction with any enemies they may have provoked, leads to their near extinct status.

6.2.6 The Fundamental Theorem of the Bonus System

In most financial institutions, there is a specific time of the year when employees will be rewarded with annual bonuses (promotions may or may not be at the same time). Broadly speaking, for employees with little experience (say less than three years) bonuses are generally a percentage (<100%) of the base salary. Employees with more experience (say more than five years), can have bonuses that are multiples of their base salary (eg, 1.25x, 2x, etc). Notwithstanding, most bonuses generally depend on three key factors[61]:

– Your performance (eg, achievements, contributions, etc)
– Your business unit's performance
– The overall firm's performance

The weighting of any one factor varies between firms, business lines, and managers. There are some specific, but rare, cases where some people's bonuses

---

61   Note that these criteria are through the lens of your manager, so his biases or preferences will matter as well.

are based on formulaic payouts. These formulas are usually a straight percentage of sales or profits they bring in, but this is largely reserved for very senior employees, if any. In my experience, this is very rare and most bonuses are based on some combination of the above factors.

There is one overriding approach that most managers follow when assessing each employee's bonus. It is so widely used that I call it the fundamental theorem of the bonus system:

For each employee, a manager will almost always ask himself "How little can we pay them so that they do not leave?"

This naturally assumes that they want to keep you onboard. If that is not the case, managers usually flag some issues with the employee in the evaluation/appraisal system and follow up with a disappointing bonus figure. It is their method of encouraging that employee to leave. The reason for the negative appraisals is to reduce liability and defend the lower than average bonus figures if questioned.

As much as you hope management would pour over your achievements and contributions, dividing up the numbers is a burden on management time and less likely to get the attention it deserves. As a corollary to the above theorem, making your (bonus related) desires known generally works in your favor unless you are unreasonable. My guess is that most people are afraid to broach the topic, so the few who do probably get their bonus numbers at least rounded up if not significantly boosted. When you do not speak up, your manager may be inclined to think you will not complain or leave if disappointed, and thus set the bar lower for your bonus. When discussing such sensitive topics with your manager, it is best to do this in a matter of fact, unemotional manner, keeping in mind your manager will have a informational advantage (ie, he is privy to the bonus pool figure out of which yours comes from).

So how much is unreasonable? You may be surprised. I have not been privy to huge samples of bonus data, just those figures for myself and my team. However, I have used headhunters on many occasions and they have provided some additional, though sometimes questionable, data points. The table below is a very rough guide to compensation packages in the first few years of a financial career in a standard sales and trading role.

I would caveat the numbers in two ways: investment bankers working in primary markets generally work more hours and (most) weekends and are likely to see figures slightly higher than those in the table. Those working in buy-side firms (especially hedge funds), on proprietary trading desks, and some market making desks might follow a more "do or die" theme. If their trading is very profitable, they could see higher figures as well. However, if their business has troubles or loses money, they could get nothing. The same thing could be said of people in sales who are charged with bringing in sales based revenue.

Figure 20: Approximate Total Compensation Ranges for Junior Finance Professionals (US$1,000)

Pertinent, full-time experience (yrs)	Educational background		
	BS	MS	PHD
0	75-125	125-200	125-200
1	125-175	150-225	150-225
2	150-250	200-300	200-300

Keep in mind that these numbers vary between firms and types of institution (eg, bank versus hedge fund) and are estimates based on my experience. Headhunters have huge databases filled with such information and will share information with you, but you must take into account their motives. They may want you to think you are underpaid so you will think about changing jobs or they may want you to think pay levels are lower so you will be more likely to accept lower offers.

Quick comment: As we mentioned before, compensation packages for graduate hires are standardized at most large firms; there is usually no negotiating. There may be some differences between banks, but they should not be huge. HR departments actively research competitors' compensation levels to make sure their scale is competitive and attract quality candidates. This is not necessarily the case in smaller firms.

6.2.7 Career Mobility and Changing Roles Within a Firm

Despite making all of the right efforts, it is often the case that one does not get an offer for the job they really prefer or their job does not turn out to be quite what was expected. Whatever the reason, many people seek to transition into other roles and must carefully consider career mobility. Indeed, some people might integrate this factor into their criteria for choosing any job.

Changing roles within a firm is delicate situation that should be handled with care. Whether you just started in a new group or have been there for years, moving into another role can be a challenging process. There are generally two major hurdles when it comes to making such a transition: your current manager and your potential new manager.

Provided you are a valued employee, your manager will have a vested interest in keeping you. If your manager really wants the best for you, he will explain the pros and cons of the move but ultimately will not stand in your way. If you believe your manager is really looking out for you and your best interests, you might consider being open with him and trying to work out the best mutually agreeable solution.

If your manager is overly business focused or egotistical, it is probably not in your best interest to approach him initially. You will have to be cautious, even covert, as you look around for another role in the firm. The last thing you want is for your manager to find out you are looking, especially early on when you probably do not actually have anything lined up.

When you are looking around, make sure that confidentiality is agreed before you open the door to further discussions or interviews. Eventually, if you find a role someone would like to hire you for, you should make absolutely sure it is a go before confronting your manager with the bad news. He may still protest and escalate matters to HR, but that is not the most likely scenario. Instead, he will likely capitulate with the caveat that you stay around to help him make the transition. Depending on several variables such as the relative seniority of your new manager to your current, your own seniority, and the urgency of your future versus current role, this transition time could vary from days to months.

Another factor to consider is that any potential new manager may simply prefer to hire graduates with no experience. While this may not sound meritocratic, there are logical reasons managers prefer to hire non-transition candidates. There is often a question mark around why this person ended up in a role they do not like. Maybe there is a problem with the person? Will they want to move out of my team down the road? Internal transitions can also create political issues between managers if one views the other as stealing their employee. HR generally does not encourage internal moves either, partly because of these reasons, but also because they do not want to set precedents that encourage too many others to pursue jobs where they think the grass in greener.

> **One common example:** I have seen many instances of people wanting to transition from IT into front office roles (trading primarily but also into my research team). Personally, I am particularly respectful of IT backgrounds because of their analytical nature. But in my experience, there have been few successful moves relative to the number trying. I think the primary reasons are as above, but I also get the impression that banks attach a stigma to IT employees. They are often viewed as commoditized resources. Right or wrong, this provides another headwind.

6.2.8 Resigning From Your Firm

Ideally, your current job would be the right one and it would reward you as you see fit. Realistically, this is not always the case. Employees, including junior analysts, often find themselves unhappy in their current roles. If an internal move is not possible or would not resolve the problem, then it makes sense to find a job outside the firm. Naturally, you should not let on that you are looking for another job.

If you are certain you want to leave and have secured an offer from another firm, you should stick to your guns when you walk into the room and give your resignation to your manager[62]. Clearly convey that you have made up your mind and your resignation is just a formality. This will help make the process quicker and involve less stress.

Be prepared for a show once you indicate that you are thinking about resigning. It will trigger a series of events that are essentially choreographed. Assuming they do not want you to go, they will act shocked. Really? What is the problem? We thought you were happy. The works. They will shower you with

---

62   Assuming there are no outstanding issues already, it is poor taste to resign via email or to HR first. It is respectful to inform your direct line manager first.

praise and adoration until you blush. They will tell you about big ideas they had in mind for you. They will tell you exactly why it is the worst time to make a move. They will parade senior managers in front of you to tell you that you have been on their radar. The whole idea is to butter you up, make you think it was all a misunderstanding, it won't happen again, they'll look out for you now, etc. It will be hard not to be flattered, but no matter what transpires, you should stick to your game plan to resign.

> **Quick comment:** If you are thinking about leaving your firm, there were probably some good reasons for you wanting to move and you are looking forward to starting a new opportunity. If money was the reason you started looking for another job (ie, you were disappointed with your compensation), your firm might throw more money at you. But do not forget that it took extreme measures (threatening to resign) to get the firm to pay you fairly. You might get a quick fix but still face similar issues with future bonuses.

If you are open to staying, do not show your hand too quickly. Also make up your mind as to what solutions you would find acceptable beforehand so that you are better prepared to negotiate. You could simply state that you are planning to resign if they cannot come up with a solution to make you happy. At most, let them know which solutions are possible, be it monetary, more responsibility, or moving to another group. Then let them propose solutions. You will likely be negotiating the potential solutions very quickly.

All of this assumes that you are in good standing and they would like you to stay if possible. If they do want you to go, you probably already knew it. In this case, they will go through some but not all of the same motions, albeit with less sincerity. For example, they might not waste senior managers' time to participate. Nevertheless, they will generally tell you they really enjoyed working with you and that you will be missed. However, their intention would be more to end things on a good note and avoid any potential lawsuits or other issues rather than really make you stay. Ultimately they will shake your hand and send you over to HR.

Recommended Resources

Books (author)	Category	Description
Monkey Business (John Rolfe and Peter Troob)	Investment banking	Lighthearted description of the lives (or lack of) of two investment bankers
Barbarians at the Gate (Bryan Burrough and John Helyar)	Investment banking	In depth story of bankers competing for a mega deal where egos and greed became the dominant drivers
Den of Thieves (James B. Stewart)	IB / Sales and trading	Well told story of the junk bond saga that left several bankers behind bars
Liar's Poker (Michael Lewis)	Sales and trading	Inside look at the business from the training room to the top position on a wild trading floor
Fiasco (Frank Partnoy)	Sales and trading	Detailed accounts of dubious transactions enacted by greedy bankers
The Bucks Stop Here (Jim Parton)	Sales and Trading	Humorous and self deprecating depiction of one useless salesman's well paid career of doing nothing
City Boy (Geraint Anderson)	Research	One equity researcher's very cynical look back over his own wild career with some very useful insights
Hedgehogging (Barton Biggs)	Investment management	An objective look at the investment industry covering the many trends and persona in the industry
Fooled by Randomness (Nassim Taleb)	Risk	Arrogant but accurate description of risk taking business where many confuse their luck for skill
The Excel Bible and Power Programming with VBA (John Walkenbach)	Productivity	Two excellent books to introduce one to the power of Microsoft Excel and VBA
How to Win Friends and Influence People (Dale Carnegie)	Personal skills	A classic book. Not nearly offensive as the title might suggest, it is an easy read that has helped many people with various aspects of interpersonal communications.
Fixed Income Mathematics (Frank Fabozzi)	Technical reference	Fabozzi's books have longstanding been the reference of choice for many newbies and practioners alike.
Futures, Options, and other Derivatives Securities (John Hull)	Technical reference	Virtually required reading. Good but over popularized text to introduce derivatives and the models behind them.
Dynamic Hedging (Nassim Taleb)	Technical reference	Both provide more technical and in depth derivatives modeling concepts.
Principles of Financial Engineering (Salih Neftci)	Technical reference	

Websites	Utility
Websites of banks and other financial institutions	▪ Rich source of information about individual firms and careers ▪ Online applications
www.careers-in-finance.com	▪ Industry overview ▪ Insights and strategies for job hunting
www.wilmott.com	▪ Jobs forum, albeit for more experienced hires ▪ Technical forum for mathematical finance topics
www.analyticrecruiting.com	▪ Broad albeit confusing array of job listings ▪ Much quant focus
www.efinancialcareers.com	▪ Large database of jobs (and resumes) ▪ Finance focus ▪ Other helpful tools
www.monster.com	▪ Large database of jobs (and resumes) ▪ All sorts of jobs ▪ Other helpful tools
Websites of recruiting agencies[63]	▪ Good source of information about roles available ▪ Often describe precise requirements and desired skill sets

---

63   We do not provide an exhaustive list of recruiting agencies, but you can find them by perusing the job listings in the other websites we have listed. They often post jobs to these sites.

Chapter 6 Concepts

- Internships are great
- PhD and Ivy League focus
- Networking and internal contacts
- Networking resources
- Targeted resumes and cover letters
- Following up
- Group assessments
- Interview strategies
- The hiring and final selection processes
- Working with a new manager
- Find a mentor
- Self promotion and your profile
- Internal resources
- **Fundamental theorem of the bonus system**
- Career mobility
- Changing roles within your firm
- How to resign

Appendix A:

Shorting and Leverage

Short Selling

One is said to be *long* a security (or market) if they own it and thus make money when it goes *up*. One is said to be *short* a security (or market) if they make money when it goes *down*. There are two primary ways investors can be long or short a security: having a position in the security directly or owning a derivative that gives them long or short exposure. An example of the latter could be a call (put) option where the owner benefits if the underlying security goes up (down) in value. We explain these derivatives in Appendix B: Four Very Common Derivatives.

Being long via owning a security is a relatively common concept, but being short is probably not. The following diagram and paragraph should help explain this concept and how it is accomplished via a process called *short-selling*.

Figure 21: Short Selling Diagram

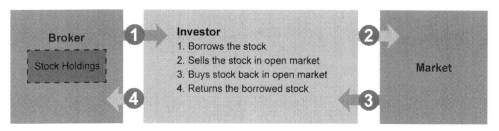

The process of shorting essentially involves four steps. The process we describe here is with respect to stocks but can be generalized to other assets. The first step is to literally *borrow* the stock from somebody else who owns it. This usually entails the broker asking its *stock lending* desk (a desk that borrows and lends stocks) to find the security to borrow. Perhaps another client of the same broker owns it or they may have to contact another stock lending desk.

It is worth noting that some stocks are more difficult to borrow than others. Indeed, those that are difficult to borrow are often referred to as *hot*. That is, there is some outstanding reason that many people want to borrow the stock and there is little supply left to borrow from. For example, the acquiring company in a big merger is usually hot because there are many risk arbitrage desks trying to short it (and purchase the company being acquired). In any case, a market develops around stock lending whereby investors pay *borrow rates* to the lender until they return the stock. This can vary from nothing to high percentages in extreme cases, but the norm is more like 10 or 20 basis points (hundredths of a percent) annualized.

Once the stock is found and borrowed, the second step is to actually sell the stock. This is done just as one would sell a holding they already have, although it is sometimes the case that there is an *up tick* rule whereby shorting is not allowed until after an up tick (ie, stock price trades at a higher price than the previous trade). This is to prevent preying on or causing panic selling.

The next step is to buy the stock back. If this is at a lower price than it was sold, then the investor makes a profit on this transaction (as long as this profit exceeds the borrow cost). In any case, this leads to the final step whereby the stock is returned to the lender.

There are two primary applications for shorting securities:

- To speculate on securities or markets going down in value. Many investors spend time identifying securities or markets that are likely to fall if not crash completely. In the world of stocks, many investors specifically look for companies that are faltering or on the brink of collapsing and take short positions in those stocks. As the world is naturally long those shares (they had to be sold/issued before they could be shorted!), people often loathe short sellers whose selling pressures depress the values of their securities. People sometimes get worried and sell their own securities when they sell off significantly. In this case there can sometimes be a snowball effect on the downside as more people sell their holdings.
- To employ relative value strategies where one is long one asset and short another (usually related or correlated) asset. The strategy does not benefit from overall markets going up or down as both assets would rise and fall, canceling out any gains or losses. Instead, the strategy profits when the

long asset goes up more than the short asset or goes down less than the short asset. The merger situation above is one such example. Consider for example, an investor believes stock A is cheap and stock B is expensive and expects for them to revert back to their fair values. He establishes a long position in A and short position in B. If asset A and B go up by say 3% and 2%, respectively, then the investor will make more money on A than he will lose on B. If asset A and B go down by say 2% and 3%, respectively, then the investor will lose less money on A than he will make on B. Moreover, if A were to go up and B were to go down, he would profit on both legs; that would be the ideal situation. However, the worst situation would be if A were to go down B were to go up as he would lose on both legs.

Leverage

Intuitively, one might define *leverage* as taking on more risk exposure than there is capital. That is, a leveraged position would allow for the loss of not only the capital employed, but potentially more. Margin systems such as those employed by brokerages are setup to facilitate leverage. Indeed, investors need only post enough capital to satisfy the margin requirement for their positions; the broker lends them the rest. If, for example, the margin requirement was only 20% of the position size, an investor could leverage his capital five times. Naturally, this allows for greater profits, but it also entails the risk of larger losses.

Many people associate derivatives with leverage and there is fair reason to do so. For starters, futures contracts that trade on exchanges are margined and thus allow for leverage. However, it is the nature of the application that really determines if one is leveraged or not. For example, a farmer who wishes to lock in the current price level for his harvest (eg, sugar, cotton, wheat, etc) may sell futures (note: this is the original motivation for futures). If these futures do not exceed the size of his crops, is that really leverage? Financially, he could lose more than he sold them for if the price more than doubled. However, in this instance, the transaction has been used for hedging purposes (by the farmer), not speculation. On the other side of the transaction, perhaps there is a speculator who buys the futures. This person may or may not have purchased them on margin. Accordingly, whether leverage is being used essentially depends upon the application and capital used to finance a position.

This raises the question of whether shorting is really leveraging or not. In theory, you can lose more money than a position is actually worth when shorting. The price simply has to go up by more than 100%. As a result, many people claim that portfolios that entail short positions are leveraged. However, one could argue that being long one security and short another related security actually reduces risk. Indeed, this is generally the case in practice. Consider a fully financed long position which is, of course, not leveraged. The addition of a complementing short position may involve leverage on a theoretical basis (actually unlimited risks), but most brokers will view this as being less risky and thereby actually decrease margin requirements for the combined position.

Lastly we consider the case of vanilla call and put options (*Appendix B: Four Very Common Derivatives* describes these products in more detail). Just as with futures, labeling transactions as leveraged or not depends on the context. Consider the case where one purchases options; the risks are unlimited to the upside[64] while the investor can only lose the capital used to purchase the options, nothing more. However, the options can end up being worth nothing. Compare this to where the capital is used to purchase the underlying assets (eg, stocks or bonds) instead. These assets may fluctuate in value but generally will not end up worthless – at least not as often as options.

Thus, an investor who purchases options instead of the actual assets is taking much greater risks (upside and downside). Options are inherently leveraged since they give investors the exposure to a larger notional. Accordingly, the capital used to purchase options should be on the same order of magnitude as the investor's risk or loss tolerance. For example, an investor with $100 to invest might use $10 of it to purchase call options on an equity index and place the rest in a risk-free bond. This particular example is often packaged together and offered as a structured product[65].

---

64   Actually the put option has limited upside since the underlying asset generally cannot go below zero.

65   Interested readers can lookup "capital guaranteed products". For a $100 investment and a given time horizon, just enough money is placed in zero coupon bond so that it will be worth $100 at expiry. The rest of the money (which depends upon the level of interest rates) is then used to purchase (call) options which give upside exposure to a particular asset or index. Even if the option expires worthless, the bond component makes sure the investor gets his original investment of $100 back. This may look good on the surface but it sacrifices the interest and dividends one would normally receive by investing directly the cash assets.

Selling options is slightly different. For example, selling puts is effectively the same as an insurance company selling policies. If the seller does not have the capital to backup the potential payout, this is certainly a leveraged position (akin to the insurance company not being able to pay its claims). On the other hand, selling calls is similar to short selling. Unless the seller holds the underlying asset and can deliver it (just as a farmer who sells futures could), this would also be a leveraged transaction.

Four Very Common Derivatives

Here we describe four of the most popular types of vanilla derivatives: futures, options, interest rate swaps, and credit default swaps. Our goal is to provide a brief description that conveys the mechanics and some applications of each product.

Futures

Futures were originally conceived in the context of allowing farmers to lock in prices for their goods, be it a crop or animal product. A future, as the name indicates, is essentially an agreement to buy or sell something at a future point in time. The product must be well defined (so there is not bait-and-switch) and then the price, quantity, and time are also specified. In this case, the seller generally delivered the product to the buyer at expiry. This is called *physical settlement*. However, as futures have been used for increasing broader purposes, a *cash settlement* process has evolved to avoid the cumbersome physical delivery. Instead, the buyer pays the seller the difference between the specified future and spot price, which could be negative. If the buyer so wished, they could then purchase the asset at the spot (current) price, which would work out to the same as if it were a physical delivery since they would receive the asset and have paid the future price. In summary, the buyer paid spot for the asset and (future – spot) to the futures seller; so the total works out to the original future price.

The pricing mechanism for futures is based on the cost of hedging. In particular, the price is generally equal to the cost of borrowing the money to purchase the asset, plus the cost of storage, minus any dividends or interest the asset might provide before expiry. The price of the future, which entitles ownership to the asset at a specified date in the future, will not reflect expectations of where the asset price will be at that time. Instead, its price will be determined in such a way that nobody can arbitrage the future against the asset.

For example, consider a 3-month future on a stock that yields no interest or dividends. Let's suppose the stock costs $100 today and interest rates are 4%. In this case, the future will be priced at $101; any other price will lead to an arbitrage situation. If the future trades at a price of $102, someone can borrow $100 and purchase the asset today, then deliver it in three months time for $102, pay back their loan $100 + $1 of interest (4% pro-rated for three months), and have a dollar leftover as profit. Conversely, someone could execute the reverse transaction if the future traded below $101.

Figure 22: Future Replication and Pricing

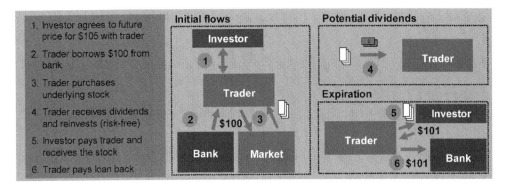

In this case, we assumed no dividends; but if there was a $1 dividend, it would serve to reduce the future price by that amount. Technically, the dividend cash could be invested risk-free for some extra interest and that total would be the amount by which to reduce the future price. Taking this one step further, the stock could be lent out and the borrow fees would also reduce the future price.

For our stock example, storage is not an issue since it is ultimately done electronically. However, in the case of commodities, not only is it the case that the underlying assets do not provide any dividends or interest, but there is also a cost of storage. Thus, in the replication where one purchases the underlying security, it must been be physically stored somewhere and this costs money. As a result, the future price is generally higher than the spot price, all else equal.

Options: Call and Puts

A *call option* gives the holder the right but not the obligation to purchase the underlying asset at a fixed price (the *strike price*) over a pre-specified time period. A *put option* gives the holder the right but not the obligation to sell the underlying asset at a fixed price (the *strike price*) over a pre-specified time period. When an investor chooses to take advantage of this right, they are said to *exercise the option*. Naturally, one will only exercise their option if it makes economic sense. That is, a call (put) option will only be exercised if the market price is higher (lower) than the strike price at expiry. It is important to know that some options allow for early exercise and others only at expiration. The former are called American and the latter European options. In most cases the option are paid for upfront and the cost is generally referred to as the option *premium*. A *straddle* is the combination of a long call and long put position and is illustrated in Figure 23.

Figure 23: Call, Put and Straddle Payouts (strike prices = 100)

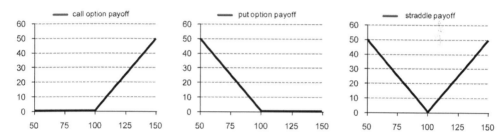

At any point in time the difference between the spot price and the strike price is called the *intrinsic value* of a call option; it is the amount of money the option would be worth if it were exercised immediately. In the case of a put, it is the strike minus the spot price. Options with a positive intrinsic value are said to be *in-the-money* (ITM). Options where the strike price is equal to the spot price are said to be *at-the-money* (ATM). Options with a negative intrinsic value are said to be *out-of-the-money* (OTM). Defined this way, intrinsic value is always non-negative.

Intrinsic value is one component of an option price; the other component is *time value*. This refers to the value the option derives from potentially having a higher intrinsic value at some point before expiry. Only in extreme cases can time value be negative (eg, a put where the asset price is near zero).

There is a precise relationship that exists between the price of call and put options (ie, those on the same underlying with the same maturity and strike). In particular, a short put option and long call option replicates a forward (future) position in the underlying asset – it makes money if the underlying goes up (via the long call) and loses if it goes down (via the short put). As a result, the present value of both positions must be the same since the payout is the same. This relationship is called *put-call parity*. Dividends and interest rates also play a role in this relationship but we have brushed them under the rug for the sake of simplicity.

Another interesting relationship that is observed with options is that ATM option prices vary approximately linearly with respect to implied volatility. While this may be shown mathematically (several terms cancel out in the Black-Scholes formula), the reader might find it an interesting exercise to reason this out intuitively.

We do not discuss the pricing of options here as it is already well covered by many books and on the internet. We have also already described many of the greek sensitivities in Chapter 5. However, we do provide a brief introduction to the concept of trading volatility since it is not as well known. In particular, we illustrate how vanilla options can be used to *trade volatility* via several simplified examples.

The first and easiest way to illustrate this is to consider an ATM straddle on an asset. The payoff diagram looks like the letter "v". An investor who owns such a position does not necessarily care if the market goes up or if it goes down. He simply wishes that it moves significantly in either direction since he will then profit in the option that is ITM (ie, the option he could exercise and earn a profit). Here the investor has a non-directional view but simply wishes for volatility in one direction or another. In other words, he is *long volatility*. Conversely, an investor with the opposite position (ie, a short straddle) naturally wants the underlying asset not to move so that he does not have to pay much when the holder of the options exercises the one that ends up ITM. This investor is said to be *short volatility*.

The "v" shaped payout we described above represents the payout at maturity. Before then, we must use a derivatives pricing model to value the options in the interim. The resultant diagram looks more like a symmetric bowl that fits within the "v". Note that the value of an option is generally greater than its intrinsic value (ie, there is time value), so the option value will be higher than the payoff value.

Figure 24: Straddle Payout and Pricing Diagram

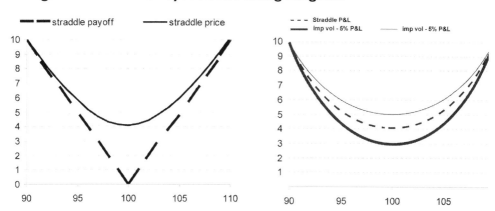

Note: While we use an ATM straddle, any option can be delta hedged so that its price chart looks symmetric just as above.

Recall that increases in the implied volatility of an option increase the value of the option. Accordingly, if the implied volatility of the options above were to increase, the prices of the options would increase, and the "bowl" would move higher, thus indicating a profit. On the other hand, if implied volatility were to decrease, the "bowl" would sink and result in a loss. Thus we can see that delta hedged options can be used to monetize views on the direction of implied volatility.

The last angle we consider here is gamma. While most textbooks define gamma as the change in delta per unit move in the underlying, it has a more practical definition in practice. In particular, gamma is generally used to describe one's exposure to *realized volatility*. The connection is relatively easy to make. Gamma is the second derivative of the option price with respect to the underlying. In terms of the diagram above, this indicates the amount of convexity there is in the "bowl".

For the long straddle position (or any delta hedged option), the position will profit if the underlying goes up or down as the price increases as it climbs along the edge of the bowl. When there is more gamma, the bowl will be more convex and the investor will profit quicker per unit move in the underlying.

Figure 25: Implied and Realized Volatility P&L

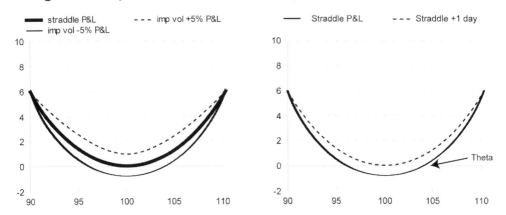

Note: These charts represent P&L (change in the value of the options)

However, (positive) gamma comes with a cost. It simply would not make sense if you could make money if markets go up or down with no downside. What does not show up in the first panel of Figure 25 is time; it is only a snapshot. The second panel shows the straddle P&L after one day has lapsed. The time to maturity is now decreased so the option value decreases accordingly. The amount by which it decreases is *theta*. Some people refer to theta as *gamma rent* because it is effectively the daily price of maintaining gamma exposure.

Interest Rate Swaps

In order to understand interest rate swaps, one must first understand the concepts of fixed and floating rates. For a variety of different reasons that generally revolve around managing the economy, or supply and demand, interest rates fluctuate over time. When corporations (or people) borrow or lend money, they can choose to either *fix* the interest rate or let it *float*. In the case of fixed interest rates, the coupon or interest payments will be fixed throughout the life of the loan; they are usually quoted as a fixed interest rate, but the notional does not change so the actual payments are fixed as well. For a floating rate, however, the interest payments are made in accordance with the prevailing level of interest rates when the payments are made; the interest rate floats with current market levels.

Clients often wish to convert their fixed payments to floating or vice versa. Sometimes they also want to change the currency in which they pay. Interest rate swaps are OTC derivative contracts that accomplish precisely this.

Figure 26: Interest Rate Swap Example Diagram

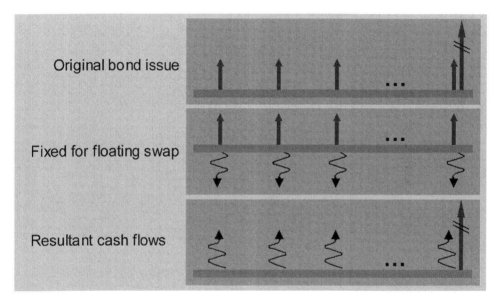

When a swap is initiated, it usually has a net present value of zero. That is, discounting both legs of the swap produces the same value. In order to make this possible, a spread will be added to or subtracted from the floating rate to equalize that floating leg with the fixed leg. For example, consider a corporation that is making fixed 8% payments on a 10 year $1,000 bond who would like to convert their payments to floating. If current market rates are lower, say around 5%, than the 8% they are already paying, the swap's floating payments will be expressed as a floating rate + 300 bps (3%). This is just an approximation but the spread should essentially reflect the difference between the fixed rate and what markets are currently pricing in.

Most of the mathematics behind interest rate swaps is no more complex than that of basic bond math. Currency conversions, day count conventions, and other features can make the calculations more tedious, but the required mathematics are still relatively simple.

Credit Default Swaps

A credit default swap (CDS) is an OTC contract is essentially an insurance policy with respect to the credit of an underlying company. The purchaser pays a running fee (quoted as an annual percentage of the notional being "insured") and the seller agrees to a payout in the case of a default or bankruptcy (or in some cases a restructuring). Just as with options, the payout can be physical or cash settlement. It is also worth noting that the buyer's method of payment is a running fee, not an upfront premium (like an option). Moreover, this fee is paid up until maturity or a default, whichever comes first.

Figure 27: Credit Default Swap Diagram

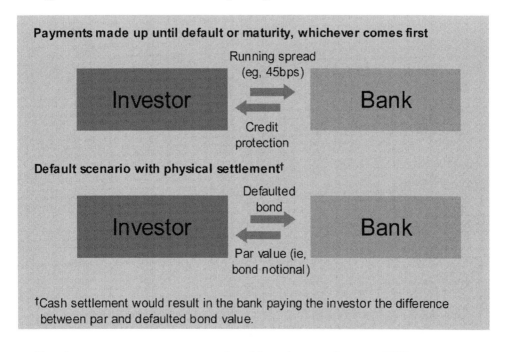

If an investor owns a corporate bond but also purchases a CDS to protect against defaults or bankruptcy of that company, the position should roughly equate to a risk-free bond. Recall that corporate bonds pay an extra *credit spread* to compensate investors for risks (eg, default and a risk premium). But this credit spread will be approximately equal to the running cost of the CDS. As a result, the extra premium is paid away for the protection and the investor is left with a yield that should be comparable to risk-free (eg, government) bonds.

Looking at this from another perspective, one can create a *synthetic* corporate bond by packaging a risk-free bond together with a short CDS position. The short CDS will provide extra yield just like a normal corporate bond and it will also suffer in the case of default since the investor in this package would have to pay to settle (or physically settle) the insurance payment.

It is also interesting to note that one does not have to own the bond in order to purchase the insurance. CDS may be purchased (or sold) for speculative rather than protective purposes. As a result, there has been little to prevent the size of the CDS market for a given corporate to overtake the size of the underlying corporate bond market. In the case of default, this could lead to problems if there are too many contracts based on physical delivery since there would not be enough bonds to deliver.

Appendix C:

The Collateralized Debt Obligation (CDO)

CDOs are just one example of an asset backed security (**ABS**). In particular, we describe a generic structure that is collateralized by corporate bonds (debt) but there are many other types of assets that are structured in the same way (eg, mortgages, credit cards debts, auto loans, etc).

Basic Description

In a regular (mutual) fund, investors have fractional ownership of a pool of assets. Everyone will profit or lose by the same percentage, though this will be more (less) for investors who own a larger (smaller) share in the fund. This amounts to owning a *vertical* slice of assets as illustrated in the first panel below.

Figure 28: CDO diagrams

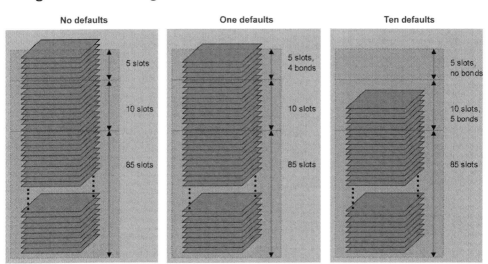

Now let's consider the same "stack" of assets but where ownership is split up in a different manner. In particular, instead of holding vertical slices, investors in a CDO will hold horizontal slices. For simplicity, we will assume there are 100 bonds and we will divide this stack into three horizontal slices corresponding to three different investors.

Going from the top to bottom, let's say the heights of these horizontal slices (as represented by the number of bonds stacked within) are 5, 10, and 85 for a total of 100 bonds. In practice, the horizontal slices are called *tranches* and the borders that define the size of each tranche are called *detachment points*; they are usually expressed as percentages of the size of the original portfolio (eg, 0-5%, 5-10%, etc). The top tranche here is called the *equity tranche*, the middle is called the *mezzanine tranche*, and the bottom is the *senior tranche*[66].

Now envisage that each time a bond defaults, the horizontal sliver representing that bond will collapse and the overall stack will become shorter. For simplicity, we assume a zero recovery rate so that a bond goes to zero upon default. Thus, in the case of the first default, when the equity (top) tranche holder looks into his horizontal slice, he will see that it is no longer full. Indeed, after one bond defaults, the stack is only 99 high and his horizontal slice which was five tall is now only occupied by four bonds (there is one slot empty). As a result, he loses 20% of his principal (one slice out of the five). This is illustrated in the second panel of Figure 28.

Now, this may sound harsh especially since the mezzanine and senior tranche holders suffered no loss. However, the tranches are naturally priced according to the risks. The equity tranche is the cheapest and the senior tranche is the most expensive. So the yield on the equity tranche is highest and it is lowest for the senior tranche.

The only way for the mezzanine tranche to suffer a loss is if more than five bonds default. At that point, the equity tranche has lost all of its principle[67] (five out of five) and the losses are starting to impact the mezzanine tranche as the stack gets shorter and shorter. For example, if ten bonds default, the

---

66   My illustration and stacking example is upside down relative to most others' depictions. I did it this way so that I could use the concept of gravity in my intuitive "stacking" example as it related to how losses are distributed.

67   Though it may have received some interest payments.

equity tranche is wiped out and five of the ten mezzanine slots are gone now as well. This is illustrated in the third panel of Figure 28. As the mezzanine tranche was originally ten tall, this represents a loss of 50% to the mezzanine tranche. Similarly, if 20 bonds defaulted, this wipes out both the equity and mezzanine tranches and incurs a loss of 5.9% (5 out of 85 slots gone) to the senior tranche.

While it is easy to get caught up in these details, there is something very important happening here. In particular, banks and other institutions have been able to take assets of varying credit quality (even so called "junk" bonds), restructure their payouts in this format, and create assets of a higher credit quality (well, at least with higher ratings). The total risk is the same but more of it is concentrated in the equity and mezzanine tranches. They both serve as buffers for the senior tranche as it will not get hit until they are completely wiped out themselves. The more buffer there is (ie, the larger the size of the equity and mezzanine tranches), the more protected the senior tranche is since it requires more losses before it is affected.

These senior tranches could be structured so that the resultant risk was low enough (ie, the buffer was large enough) to earn them an investment grade rating. These products generally had higher yields than other investment grade bonds. As a result, they appeared to be attractive alternatives for the various pension funds and insurers who actively purchased "safe" investment grade products for their portfolios.

We have brushed several details under the rug here but have presented the basic mechanics behind CDOs in general. They are structured in different ways and the assets behind them vary. For example, there are often more tranches (eg, a super senior) and sometimes the assets are synthetic rather than cash assets (recall the synthetic bonds we constructed in the last section of Appendix B: Four Very Common Derivatives).

One View on the Credit Crisis

I have two views that are not often reflected in popular media. First, CDOs are not bad in and of themselves. And second, banks are effectively being used as scapegoats; governments and regulators do not fully own up to their responsibility.

CDO technology, which is often blamed for the recent turmoil or credit crisis, is actually a quite innovative and useful tool. It was unquestionably abused and has caused huge problems around the globe, but in my view this is more the fault of the user rather than the product itself. Banks were not the only users and it was actually the government who popularized (and also abused) this technology.

Indeed, it should be noted that the US government originally setup the system whereby banks could offload their risks (ie, mortgages) via establishing the Fannie Mae in the post depression era and Freddie Mac some 50 years later. These institutions bought these risky assets, repackaged them using CDO technology, and sold them onto investors hungry to buy investment grade assets, booking healthy profits in the process.

In recent decades, this business seemed almost untouchable. On the one hand, the government encouraged (lending) banks to underwrite mortgage risks they might not otherwise approve via efforts such as the Community Reform Act. On the other hand, the government, via regulators, forced many investors (eg, pensions, which manage the largest pool of money in the world) into investment grade assets. Investment banks saw that they could make billions of dollars repackaging these risks and got into the game. Place a slab of meat at the edge of your lawn and it should not be surprising if your neighbor's dog eats it. A dog's instinct for food is not dissimilar to a banker's instinct for money. Notwithstanding, few people would disagree that the banks abused this technology and took on far too much risk that eventually led to their collapse (as did Fannie Mae and Freddie Mac). In hindsight, it is clear that regulators should have been regulating what it took to receive an investment grade rating as these repackaged products ended up being far too risky.

So what was the abuse? Due to the investment grade rating and higher yields (which are usually a flag for higher risk), banks could not create and sell this repackaged risk quickly enough. They effectively ran out of bonds to repackage. At first, they started using junk bonds but then had to start creating them synthetically when the physical bonds themselves were in scarce supply. Then banks started to execute CDOs based on the higher risk tranches of other CDOs (these were called CDO^2, "CDO squared"). However, the banks were left with residual risks that kept getting larger and larger. Many banks used hedge funds to take on some of the risk, but the hedge funds generally cherry picked the most attractive risks to take on, thus leaving banks with the more toxic risks. Many of these were swept into off-balance-sheet vehicles and were not properly risk managed (ie, the banks did not hold enough capital to back them).

The Exchange Traded Fund (ETF)

ETFs have become incredibly popular over the last decade or so, and with good reason. They give investors a simple product that can provide exposure to a variety of broad indices (eg, the S&P 500). ETFs trade on exchanges just like stocks and are thus accessible to most investors. Perhaps more importantly is the fact that ETFs generally charge much lower fees than their mutual fund competition.

Historically, many investors' portfolios have not been big enough to make buying 100 or 500 stocks feasible; transaction costs would create a huge drag. As a result, many people put their money in mutual funds. Some mutual funds are *passive* and simply track a benchmark index; others are *active* funds whose managers attempt to use their stock selection skills to outperform their benchmarks. Unfortunately, many studies show that most active funds underperform their benchmarks and investors are generally better off placing their money in passive investments.

Performance aside, both passive and active mutual funds generally charge hefty fees. It would not be uncommon to find a mutual fund charging 1-4% for a front load fee just to place money with them. They also charge management and operating expense fees annually that can amount to another 1-3% in costs per year.

ETFs provide virtually the same service as passive mutual funds but generally only charge a modest annual fee, usually well below 1%. As a result, ETFs have been one of the biggest success stories of the last decade. Here we provide a brief description of the mechanics of the ETF product.

An ETF is a fund. That is, its holdings are pooled together and investors in the fund all have equal ownership. Moreover, it is an open ended fund. In other words, new shares can be created or redeemed thus making the fund's AUM (assets under management) larger or smaller. This is the opposite of a closed end fund which raises capital once and manages only that money.

There is the team who manages the actual fund. They attempt to track the benchmark index by making sure the fund holds the constituents of the index in the right proportions. They also reinvest or distribute cash flows (eg, dividends) as well as manage corporate actions (eg, merger and acquisitions) that impact the index composition. These responsibilities are more or less the same as a mutual fund manager.

The defining feature of an ETF lies within the fund's *creation* and *redemption* of its shares. Unlike mutual funds, ETFs do not accept cash for new shares and then go out and buy the stocks to increase the size of their fund. Instead, they exchange new shares *in-kind*. That is, new ETF shares are created and exchanged for a basket of stocks (that it would otherwise go out and buy). Conversely, shares are redeemed by the fund taking in and canceling shares and returning a basket of stocks (that it would otherwise go out and sell) to the redeemer. One benefit of this process is that it keeps transaction costs down since they do not need to execute multiple transactions for creation/redemption.

The creation/redemption process is limited to *authorized participants* (APs). These are usually banks or market makers. Just as with futures, arbitrage will keep the ETF trading close to its net asset value (NAV). If the price of the ETF is too low relative to the stocks it owns, the APs will purchase shares of the ETF in the open market, redeem their ETF shares for the in-kind basket of shares with the fund, and then sell those shares into the market. Since the ETF was cheaper than the value of the shares, they would make a profit. Conversely, if the ETFs were trading at a premium to the NAV, the APs would execute the opposite transaction. In any case, this arbitrage mechanism ensures that ETFs trade close to their NAV and thus provide a fair price for investors buying/selling them.

Originally ETFs were solely an equity phenomenon, but they are now used as a vehicle to trade other asset classes as well. It is worth noting that there are other products that look and feel like ETFs but are actually very different. Exchange traded notes (ETNs), for example, are not the same as ETFs; they involve taking on the credit risk of the issuer and have a more limited creation/redemption process. Investors should be careful when choosing amongst these investments.

Appendix E:

My Own Trajectory

The reason I decided to write this book is simple; it is precisely what I wish I had had when I entered the world of finance. The following describes my own trajectory into this dynamic industry.

I have always had a fondness for mathematics and ended up studying it almost exclusively throughout my academic career. While I found this pursuit challenging and enjoyable, I often wondered where my mathematical skills would take me in terms of a professional career. As more of my friends started talking about their ideas for careers, I was often haunted by a burdensome feeling since I was not able to clearly identify any for myself, let alone a career that would leverage my mathematical skills.

There were, of course, always academic paths to follow. Indeed, I could have pursued a career as a teacher or a professor[68]. However, each time I started to think about it, it seemed to me that academics fell on the wrong side of the supply/demand spectrum; the job market was overly competitive and teachers generally underpaid.

In the latter half of my high school years, I was temporarily relieved of my career choice burden when my parents introduced me to the actuarial sciences. My mother was working at an actuarial firm and observed many mathematically minded actuaries launch successful careers. Then my father dug up virtually every job ranking survey published in America at the time and most of them indicated the best career was as an actuary since it entailed low stress and high earnings.

I thought I had found the ideal job for my mathematical background, so I got started in this direction right away. I passed the first actuarial exam while in

---

68   Actually, I do not at all rule this out as I really enjoyed teaching while in graduate school and will likely return to it at some point.

high school and then got into the University of Florida (UF) to pursue degrees in mathematics and statistics. Two years and one more actuarial exam later, someone told me something that made me question my actuarial track: "Actuaries are people who thought accounting was too exciting." I asked a few professors and did my own investigating. It turned out that I had not thought too much about the "low stress" facet of the career and later decided the actuarial sciences were not for me. I started to look for something a little more exciting[69].

Back to square one with choosing career, I bought myself a time extension by signing up for a Master's degree in applied mathematics. Around that time, three things happened that all seemed to point me in the new direction of finance.

First, my mathematics department started offering a course in mathematical finance. I signed up for it and was really intrigued. It was a mathematical introduction to the widely used Black-Scholes derivative pricing framework. As I would find out later, the course only touched the surface of how mathematics was used in finance.

Second, William R Hough and Co. (a local investment bank[70]) advertised a job for a quantitative analyst. The role was in a group that did "proprietary trading in the equity capital markets." I did not really know what most of these words meant in that context at the time, but I did know that I was qualified and wanted to learn more. I really enjoyed the work and was given an unexpected, generous bonus.

And lastly, one of my best friends who had embarked on his own financial career in New York told me about "quants" in finance. After a little research on some of the headhunting websites, I saw the salaries (more specifically, the bonuses) that financial firms were paying quants.

---

69   This is not based on any actual experience other than my own investigating. In fact, I now really believe that there are exciting and challenging actuarial careers out there.

70   William R Hough and Co was a small Florida investment bank started by the very first University of Florida MBA graduate, William R Hough. It has since been acquired by Royal Bank of Canada.

So finance seemed to be an area which sought people with mathematics, engineering, physics, or other quantitative backgrounds, appeared challenging and dynamic, and paid large bonuses that were often multiples of the base salaries. I was hooked.

I applied and interviewed with several large financial institutions in New York and two things immediately became clear. First, I still did not get the big picture of what was going on in these institutions. Indeed, I had applied to jobs that required quantitative backgrounds not really knowing exactly what the roles were. The other realization I had was that they were looking almost exclusively for PhDs at the time; my MS did not seem to measure up.

While I did receive of a couple of job offers, neither felt right. I decided to go back to UF to pursue a PhD and then make a second attempt at Wall Street. Luckily, William R Hough was kind enough to keep me on as a consultant. So I spent the next two years building and refining trading models for them while researching financial derivatives for my PhD.

As my PhD neared its end, I started hunting for a job again. I realized that my PhD, while based on financial derivatives, was quite focused and did not broaden my understanding of the industry. I would have a PhD but still no real grasp on the overwhelmingly huge financial world. I again found myself struggling as I interviewed for jobs that I did not completely grasp.

Myself, I got lucky. It turned out that my best friend's girlfriend's friend's friend (that is not a typo) was temping for the secretary to the manager who was hiring for a role that I really wanted. I finessed, if not harassed, them into hiring me. But nobody should count on luck and this is the reason I decided to write this book.

I read several books before I embarked on my Wall Street crusades. While all of them were probably accurate in covering their respective topics, I found most of them too academic or too narrowly focused. That being said, my book comprises the essential areas that both quants and non-quants who aspire to work in the financial services industry should grasp. Understanding the broader industry as well as the roles within should help immensely. Moreover, understanding how the *other side* operates will better prepare you to deal with potential employers and managers at all stages of your career.

This includes starting with your initial job search, interviewing and landing a good job, and then going on to have a successful career from there.

So it is my hope that this overview will serve to inform and better prepare others, especially those like me with quantitative background, who are investigating careers in the world of finance.

Thanks for reading,
Aaron

aaronbrask@gmail.com

Made in the USA
Middletown, DE
10 September 2021